Through the Eyes of Esther

Stepping Stones into Greatness Paved in the Path of Destiny

Dr. Michelle Corral

ISBN 978-0-9975864-9-7

Chesed Publishing

Unless otherwise stated, all Scripture quotations are taken from the King James Version (KJV) of the Bible.

DEDICATION

This book is dedicated to my beloved lifelong companion and spouse, Reverend Manuel Corral, and to the six million Jews who lost their lives in the Holocaust; their blessed memory will be remembered forever.

Introduction

The saga of Esther is more than a fairy-tale version of a captive orphan who marries the most powerful man in the world. As the gentle, passive Hadassah (Esther) makes her decision unto death, she has no idea that out of her brave choice she would emerge to be a heroine known forever as Queen Esther. Though given the name Esther on the day of her kidnapping, her preeminent greatness transpires upon her resolution to be willing to sacrifice her life for her people. It is in that moment that Hadassah becomes Queen Esther.

Following her astounding example, you can move into the pathway of promises and achieve a place of your highest potential that you never thought possible. The early life of Esther reveals one excruciating tragedy after another. Her legacy teaches us that God can take the darkest days of our lives and use them for destiny. Her heroism did not just arise in the defining moment of her decision unto death. It was her selfless love for others in the midst of her own pain that became a supernatural secret of her eminent end. It was not through her striking beauty that she triumphed to such heights of prestige and power. Her crown was not the achievement of a beauty contest. Instead, it was her deep relationship with her God. It was through her innermost intrinsic character traits. These incredible jewels that lie within her soul are based primarily on *chesed* (acts of kindness), *machshava* (deep interior thought and deliberating skill), and her incredible *sekel* (perceptiveness). Her most valuable diamond was her obedience to Mordecai.

Megillah Esther is a book of heroic greatness and inconceivable wickedness. The deplorable Amalek's device against the Jews through Haman, the son of Hamadatha the Agagite, dates back to the time of the patriarchs. Let's spiral back in time to the original conflict in the womb of Ribka (Rebecca). The violent struggle between her twins (Jacob and Esau) was not biological, but deeply spiritual. In prayer, God gave Ribka (Rebecca) the promise that the elder (Esau) would serve the younger (Jacob), meaning all the rights of land and inheritance belonged to Jacob. The battle between Esau and Jacob was more than just sibling rivalry. It resulted in the insatiable wickedness of Esau's most notorious descendant: his grandson Amalek.

In this book, you will learn the greatest Biblical success secret, and you will receive knowledge of how to develop your character traits. These are absolutely essential to reaching your highest potential and purpose. You will also learn the difference between coincidence and providence, which is the hidden hand of God directing and protecting your destiny. The Bible teaches that the evils of Amalek are in every generation. It is our responsibility to be like Esther and Mordecai to destroy Amalek in our midst. Just as Haman devised to destroy the Jews right before the rebuilding of their temple and *Shivat Zion* (return to Zion), so does Amalek attack us before our destiny.

Beloved, there are two parts to every chapter.

Part One of each chapter is "An Experience in the Megillah Through the Eyes of Esther," in which you will relive this *megillah* (scroll) with Esther through the personal perspective of her story in her very own words.

Part Two of each chapter is titled "Stepping Stones into Greatness" for learning how to build godly character from Esther's life. This section includes practical, Biblical principles of applying and developing godly character traits that open the doors of destiny in our lives.

I believe within you lies the spiritual potential and greatness of Esther and Mordecai. The blueprint to release this blessing is in God's Word. May the Lord open the door to your destiny for such a time as this.

Sincerely,
Dr. Michelle Corral+

TABLE OF CONTENTS

Chapter One

Miraculous Moments with Destiny

An Experience In the Megillah Through the Eyes of Esther:

The Moedim

The divine translation of time into destiny is the only way I can explain how the miracles of my people's deliverance happened. My Creator was hidden, yet I could see Him. He did not appear in form or configuration. Instead, He appeared through His hidden hand in divine orchestration of time and events.

He supervised our history through His ambiguity and hiddenness. He remained shrouded behind circumstances, yet the magnitude of the miracles that happened could not have occurred unless they were supernaturally orchestrated and coordinated by Him. My King directs every detail of His Kingdom. His omniscience and omnipresence are revealed when we look at the past and see His arrangement of events.

Four years before I became queen, the King of heaven began orchestrating the moves of our destiny. He brought a divine intrusion into history. King Ahasuerus was compelled to call Vashti, the queen at that time, to appear in front of the men's banquet. Vashti refused to respond to his outlandish request, which resulted in her removal from the position of queen. A search for a new queen began, and through the favor of God, I ascended the throne. These events hidden in history were part of a divine design to redeem our people. Knowing in advance the pending ploy of Haman the Agagite to destroy the children of Israel, God maneuvered and orchestrated these things for His people's sake, that I might reign in Vashti's stead.

God's orchestration of events could even be seen many years before when I was a little girl. The darkest day in my life was when the elders brought me the news that my *Ima* (Mother) and *Abba* (Father) were gone. I cried and I cried. Nothing could comfort me. All I can remember were the outstretched arms of unfamiliar kin, crying out to me, "Oh, Hadassah, Hadassah!"

In a traumatized state of being afraid, empty, and abandoned, I heard the sound of the kindest voice approaching me. It was deep and compassionate. The man's hand, though a bit rugged, tenderly brushed away my tears. In love, he shared my sorrow. He gave me kisses on my forehead and said, "Little Hadassah, I'm here now. Come, my child. I will be your father and you will be my daughter."

It was my beloved cousin, Mordecai. He was known among the people for his *chesed* (loving-kindness). He was the Torah scholar of Shushan. He taught our people the *mitzvoth* (commandments) of *Hashem* (God). Mordecai was known among our people as the *tzadik ha dor* (most righteous man). He taught me Torah. He instructed me in the ways of Hashem and the power of His providence. Mordecai taught me that our calendar is very holy, and that it was established by Hashem to tell us the times of His visitation. From the earliest times in my life, I can recall miraculous moments with destiny always colliding with the *chodeshim* (months) of the calendar. Our lives came under the rule of God's guidance, day to day, week to week, month to month, in His perfect timing.

As a child, I remember counting the sixth day of every week. It was on that day that a holy hush began to settle over us in the late afternoon. The Jewish quarter in the city of Shushan prepared for the entrance of *Shabbat* (the Sabbath) the way a city prepares for royalty. My heart beat in anxious expectancy to be the one chosen to light the candles that would welcome in the presence of Shabbat. Time would transition upon us as the flames arose and the *brachah* (blessing) was pronounced. The cup would be lifted and Hashem's world invaded our world. Shabbat was upon us. Before the meal began, Cousin Mordecai taught us that our *simcha* (joy) could never be complete because across the barren desert our holy city, *Yerushalayim* (Jerusalem), lay in ruins.

After the *kiddush* prayer, Cousin Mordecai gathered us close to the table. He spread out his *tallit* (prayer shawl) and covered his head. His voice raised in holy reverence as our Shabbat prayers were lifted for *Shivat Zion* (the return to Zion). With tears trickling down his face to his beard, he offered a *tefillah* (prayer): "How shall we sing the Lord's song in a strange land? If I forget thee, O Yerushalayim, let my right hand forget her coming."

Cousin Mordecai taught me that we were descendants of Rachel. He taught me that the weeping of my *neshama* (soul) for Shivat Zion would reach the very height of *shamayim* (heaven). He taught me how Rachel had wept for her children and refused to be comforted. He told me about the promise that Hashem had made to our mother Rachel through *Yirmiyahu HaNavi* (Jeremiah the prophet), that her tears would be rewarded and her children would again return to Zion. Hashem promised our mother Rachel that her sons and daughters, descendants of Benjamin and all of Israel, would again return to the borders of *Eretz Israel* (the land of Israel). One of the greatest sacrifices made by my beloved cousin was his offering to Hashem to stay in Shushan to take care of the Jews, even though his heart was in Zion. Every day, he would weep for the rebuilding of the walls of *Yerushalayim* (Jerusalem). Yet because of his love for our people in this *galut* (exile), Cousin Mordecai remained with us. He knew he had to stay here in Shushan to instruct our people and to keep the love of Torah alive, for many of our people had begun assimilating with the *goyim* (Gentiles). My cousin took the responsibility to strengthen our people and give them *tikvah* (hope).

It was during Shabbat, and on every *yom tov* (holy day), that Hashem demonstrated His *hashgacha pratis* (divine providence) towards us. Let me explain to you why not all time is the same.

Stepping Stones Into Greatness: *Days Filled With Destiny*

Did you know that not all time is the same? Most of us only know time as an ongoing process of days and years. It's very difficult for us to perceive time outside of a chronological concept. The Bible teaches very clearly that not all time is to be perceived only as progressive.

There are other aspects of time that God has ordained as dispensers of destiny in our lives. In Exodus 12:2, the first commandment that God gave Israel concerning the redemption out of Egypt was the command to establish a calendar.

Exodus 12:1-2 says, *"And the Lord spake unto Moses and Aaron in the land of Egypt, saying, This month shall be unto you the beginning of months: it shall be the first month of the year to you."*

God was not speaking about January when He was referring to the first month. Instead, the Almighty was commanding Israel to establish a calendar that would help them understand that, in this redemption, their days in the future would have purpose and promise. Their heavenly Father with His tender heart of mercy wanted them to know that their days would no longer be spent in toil and tears. He also wanted them to know that their souls and their destinies were going to be redeemed from *Mitzrayim* (Egypt).

You may be wondering, "What does *Mitzrayim* mean? And how do these Biblical concepts affect my destiny now?"

First of all, beloved, the Hebrew original name of the book of Exodus is *Shemot* (Names). This was the title given by Moses. During the period of postexilic Judaism, the Hebrew Scriptures were translated from Hebrew to Greek. The Greek version of the Hebrew Scriptures (the Old Testament) is called the Septuagint. The Septuagint was translated from Hebrew to Greek in the 3rd century B.C. This was done for the sake of Jews who no longer spoke Hebrew and lived in the Diaspora. In the process of translating the Bible from Hebrew to Greek, the titles of the books also changed. A change of title also means a change of concept. The Hebrew name of Exodus, which is *Shemot,* means "names."

In concept, Moses is teaching us that names are connected to our destiny. This concept is especially a predominant principle in Genesis (*Bereshit*). All of the names in Genesis are connected to an individual's prophetic purpose. For example, Abraham's original name is Abram, which means "exalted father." In Genesis 17:5, God changes his name from Abram to Abraham, meaning "A father of many nations I have made thee."

In Genesis 32:28, God changed the name of Jacob to Israel, meaning his name demonstrates a predestined destiny that his seed and land would be called "Israel." The concept of the connection between names and destiny is a major theme throughout Genesis. The book of Exodus begins with the concept that the redemptive process out of *Mitzrayim* (Egypt) includes preservation of each soul's identity and destiny.

This means that the Torah concerns itself not just with deliverance, but also with destiny. Exodus 1:1-5 says, *"Now these are the names of the children of Israel, which came into Egypt; every man and his household came with Jacob. Reuben, Simeon, Levi, and Judah, Issachar, Zebulun, and Benjamin, Dan, and Naphtali, Gad, and Asher. And all the souls that came out of the loins of Jacob were seventy souls: for Joseph was in Egypt already."*

In Exodus 1:5, there is an unusual superfluous use of the word "souls" to help us understand that the Torah is teaching not just about the physical captivity of

Mitzrayim (Egypt), but also the spiritual and emotional captivity of Mitzrayim.

The Hebrew word for Egypt, *Mitzrayim*, is not just a word that identifies a geographical location in northern Africa. *Mitzrayim* means "narrow." It denotes a place that disenables one from reaching his or her highest predestined purpose. Mitzrayim represents the limitations and bondages that keep us "stuck" behind borders that we cannot escape from. The *geulah* (redemption) out of Mitzrayim for *B'nai Israel* (children of Israel) meant one that would also release them into the highest place of promise. For years, Mitzrayim kept *B'nai Israel* (children of Israel) in a place in which all their servitude and slave labor produced no profit. Exodus 1:11 says, *"Therefore they did set over them taskmasters to afflict them with their burdens. And they built for Pharaoh treasure cities, Pithom and Raamses."*

Tenderly and compassionately, the Torah addresses our personal pain and feelings of desperation expressed in the subjugation of the children of Israel in Mitzrayim. There is no greater blow to one's human dignity than to work as hard as a slave and see that the labor does not produce profit. Mitzrayim represents 400 years of tears in backbreaking labor without producing any profit or purpose.

This is why God commanded Moses and Aaron to begin a calendar that would earmark days filled with destiny. This means God's calendar was established to redeem the time. Every day, even days of hardship and tribulation would be filled with impartation of destiny. On the calendar that God established in Exodus 12:2, He commanded that the mighty salvific works of redemption that He did during the release from Egypt would be experienced again every year during Biblical feasts.

Let us take a look into God's plan and His purposes for time. In these passages, we will see that God's divine design of destiny is executed in understanding the difference between the secular segment of time and the supernatural segment of time set in His word during the Biblical feasts.

In Genesis 1:14, the text teaches that time was created on the fourth day of creation. Genesis 1:14 says, *"And God said, let there be lights in the firmament of the heaven to divide the day from the night; and let them be for signs, and for seasons, and for days, and years."*

When we take a meticulous look at the text, we see that the last part of the verse says "for signs, and for seasons, and for days, and years." Notice that God places "signs and seasons" first before "days and years." Thus, Genesis

1:14 conveys the concept that the first and foremost highest-ranking purpose of time is marking "signs and seasons," not calculating days and years.

We understand that the highest purpose of time is to be a sign for Biblical prophecy and to proclaim the seasons.

The Biblical meaning of seasons is not weather conditions. The Hebrew word for seasons is *moedim*, which means "appointed times." These are supernatural segments of time not for commemoration, but for impartation, prophetic purpose, and destiny. God commanded that the Biblical calendar be set up for "dates with destiny." These dates with destiny are times when God has promised the expectation of divine visitation in the earth.

The Biblical calendar instructs us how to prepare for these periods of purpose and providence. Ecclesiastes 3:1 says, *"To every thing there is a season, and a time to every purpose under heaven."* "Under heaven" means coordinated and orchestrated by divine providence. These supernatural seasons or miraculous moments with destiny are so important to God that they are actually inscribed in creation and hallmark His power on earth.

God's Sign of Salvation Inscribed in Creation in The Biblical Feasts

In Genesis 1, one of the most important themes that the author wants to show us is how the Biblical feasts are not just ordinary days in a chronological secular segment of time. The intent of the author Moses is to inscribe in creation the imprint of the miracles that will occur during these miraculous moments with destiny. The divine imprint inscribed in creation also reveals that the works of God to be accomplished in the earth during these days of destiny known as the Biblical feasts were already decreed, declared, and prepared during the days of creation.

Beloved, for a moment let us review the importance of rabbinical methods of interpretation or Talmudic hermeneutics, which define the rules and methods for the investigation and exact determination of the meaning of Biblical texts. These rules of interpreting Scripture help us understand the author's intent as we investigate the book of Genesis. The Seven Middot (hermeneutical rules) of Hillel are especially useful. In the following paragraphs, we will see that the Seven Middot of Hillel show us that the Biblical feasts are inscribed in creation. In particular, we will use the second rule and the sixth rule of the Seven Middot of Hillel. The second rule is called *gezerah shevah*, and refers to similar or equivalent expressions; when we see similar words or phrases used in different parts of Scripture, we understand that these texts are connected to each other in meaning and concept. The sixth rule of the Seven Middot of Hillel is *kayotze bo mimekon akhar*, which means "analogy from another passage." Again, when we see Biblical passages that are similar to each other, we understand that they are related to each other. By using these basic rules of Talmudic hermeneutics, it will become apparent that the objective of Moses when documenting the details of creation is to demonstrate God's imprint of the Biblical feasts. All of the Biblical feasts are inscribed in creation. In particular, the three primary or pilgrimage feasts of the *Shalosh Regalim* consisting of *Pesach* (Passover), *Shavuot* (Pentecost), and *Sukkot* (Feast of Tabernacles) are inscribed in the second and third days of creation. This was done to prove that the Biblical feasts were created before time (time was created on the fourth day of creation). Therefore, the predestined salvific events that point to Calvary are shown in Genesis to be *before* time began. In Genesis 1:6-8, on the second day of creation, the Almighty inscribed the feast of Passover. It was on the second day of Passover, also known as the Feast of Unleavened Bread, that Israel left Mitzrayim and came to the Red Sea. Then God commanded Moses to stretch out his rod over the sea. Exodus 14:16 says, *"But lift thou up thy rod, and stretch out thine hand over the sea, and divide it: and the children of Israel shall go on dry ground through the midst of the sea."* Exodus 14:21 continues, *"And Moses stretched out his hand over the sea; and the Lord caused the sea to go back by a strong east wind all that night, and made the sea dry land, and the waters were divided."*

In Exodus 14:21, the last part of the verse tells us that *"the waters were **divided**."* If we compare the context in Genesis 1:6-8 on the second day of creation with the second day of Passover at the Red Sea, we will see the same exact language used.

Genesis 1:6-8 tells us, *"And God said, Let there be a firmament in the midst of the waters, and let it **divide the waters** from the waters. And God made the firmament, and **divided the waters** which were under the firmament from the waters which were above the firmament: and it was so. And God called the firmament Heaven. And the evening and the morning were the second day."*

The hermeneutical device, or tool of interpretation, is *gezerah shevah*—the rabbinic rule of interpretation that connects texts with similar words or phrases together in continuity. The appearance of similar words or phrases means that the texts are related to one another in meaning and concept. Therefore, Moses intended to connect the miracle of the Red Sea when the "waters were divided" to Genesis 1:6.

This shows us that God inscribed His revelation of Passover in the heavens on the second day of creation by dividing the waters. It shows us that Passover was designated as a day of destiny before time began. God already separated and consecrated that time to not be associated with the secular segment of time.

On the third day of creation, we can see the feast of Shavuot revealed. *Shavuot* is the Hebrew name for the Greek word "Pentecost," which is the celebration of the first fruits of the wheat harvest. Genesis 1:11-12 tells us, *"And God said, Let the earth bring forth grass, the herb yielding seed, and the fruit tree yielding fruit after his kind, whose seed is in itself, upon the earth: and it was so. And the earth brought forth grass, and herb yielding seed after his kind, and the tree yielding fruit, whose seed was in itself, after his kind: and God saw that it was good."* We can see a parallel with Leviticus 23:16, which says, *"Even unto the morrow after the seventh sabbath shall ye number fifty days; and ye shall offer a new grain offering unto the Lord."*

The word for grass is *deshe*, the herb yielding seed. *Deshe* in the Hebrew language also means "sprout." Among sprouted grains are barley and wheat. When we understand the set pattern developed in Genesis 1 by Moses, we recognize that the wheat appearing on the third day of creation is a direct connect to the feast of Shavuot which occurs during the third month on the Biblical calendar.

We can also see the Feast of Tabernacles on the third day of creation. On the third day, the tree also came forth, as we see in Genesis 1:11: *"... and the fruit tree yielding fruit after its kind."* The fruit tree prophetically parallels with the command that God gave Israel as a sign of His providence during the Feast of Tabernacles. Leviticus 23:40-41 says, *"And ye shall take you on the first day the boughs of goodly trees, branches of palm trees, and the boughs of thick trees, and willows of the brook; and ye shall rejoice before the Lord your God seven days. And ye shall keep it a feast unto the Lord seven days in the year. It shall be a statute for ever in your generations: ye shall celebrate it in the seventh month."*

We see further evidence of the Feast of Tabernacles in the seventh day of creation. Again, Moses uses the hermeneutical rule of *gezerah shevah*, to draw a comparison between the Feast of Tabernacles and the seventh day of creation. We see the word "finished" in both the creation account and in the completion of the Tabernacle in Exodus. Genesis 2:1 says, *"Thus the heavens and the earth were **finished**, and all the host of them,"* while Exodus 40:33 says, *"And he reared up the court round about the tabernacle and the altar, and set up the hanging of the court gate. So Moses **finished** the work."*

We also see the word "rested" in both the creation account in Genesis and in the description of the cloud that rested over the Tabernacle. Genesis 2:2 says, *"And on the seventh day God ended His work which He had made, and **rested** on the seventh day from all the work which He had made,"* while Numbers 10:12 tells us, *"And the children of Israel took their journeys out of the wilderness of Sinai; and the cloud **rested** in the wilderness of Paran."*

These two words, --"finished" and "rested,"-- help us understand that, when God rested, He did not take a nap because He was tired. When God rested, Moses prophetically parallels and unites the concept of rest with the cloud of glory that rested over the Tabernacle. He is demonstrating and illustrating that the first seventh day was the Feast of Tabernacles. God intended for the earth to be His Tabernacle.

We can also see Yom Kippur inscribed in creation, and we understand that God created the world with mercy in mind. In Genesis 1, Scripture shows us that God created the world in 7 days with 10 utterances. These 10 utterances of "And God said" are repetitious and are seen in Genesis 1:3, 6, 9, 11, 14, 20, 24, 26, 28 and 29. This imprint pattern of 10 and 7 appears by divine design. 10 and 7 are the symbols of Yom Kippur, or the Day of Atonement, which is the holiest day of the year on the Biblical calendar. In Leviticus 23:27, the text teaches that the Day of Atonement is the 10th day of the 7th month. This means God inscribed His mercy and forgiveness in the imprint of His creation that reflects Yom Kippur, the Day of Atonement. This Day of Atonement is God's promise that the ultimate atonement will be paid by Jesus Christ on Calvary's cross.

We see further evidence of God's signs of salvation inscribed in creation when we look at the third day of creation. The tree that came forth on the third day and the third day, itself, are symbols of the cross and resurrection. These Calvary connections tell us that God created the world with mercy in mind.

When we understand the significance of all of these signs in creation, then we understand that the Biblical feasts are categorized in a supernatural segment of time, and everyday events outside the feasts are in a secular segment of time. In the book of Esther, we see that the predestined plan of God overturns events through *hashgacha pratis* (divine providence) during the Biblical feasts.

The Hidden Hand of God: Coincidence or Divine Providence?

The primary objective in the book of Esther is to counteract coincidence. Coincidence is the concept that believes the causal connection to an event is without any divine interaction whatsoever. This means circumstances occur that God has absolutely nothing to do with. Sometimes events in our lives come by surprise. It seems as if there is a hidden hand somewhere in the background that coordinated and orchestrated what appears to be an accidental meeting, yet its effects —are surprisingly and significantly—exactly what we need. The concept of coincidence denies the divine. It refutes the reality that God in His tender care for His children has already prepared a predestined plan for everything concerning the exact details of their lives. Jesus said that *"even the very hairs of our head are numbered"* (Luke

12:7). Luke 12:6-7 further describes this divine attention to detail: *"Are not five sparrows sold for two farthings, and not one of them is forgotten before God? But even the very hairs of your head are all numbered. Fear not therefore: ye are of more value than many sparrows."*

The concept of coincidence defines God as being completely distant from the details of our lives. But our God is a loving God. His love and caring interaction that tenderly aids each person's every need is called "individual watching." Individual watching is the English term for the Hebrew concept of *hashgacha pratis* (divine providence).

On the other hand, coincidence is a concept that says there is no causal connection between events and what appears to be a "miraculous meeting." It fully removes the hidden hand of God out of the equation. How many times has an "accidental" occurrence happened in your life, that you knew had to be planned by Someone who was lovingly watching over you?

The intrinsically evil ideology that denies divine interaction between heaven and earth is the ideology of Amalek. It paints a portrait of God that is completely untrue. Our heavenly Father is very much concerned with every detail of our lives. He even responds to the most secret, private thoughts within us. He knows the very origin of our desires and needs, and His individual watching responds to it! He is not oblivious, cold, and calloused to our personal needs.

Psalm 139:4-6 says, *"For there is not a word in my tongue, but, lo, O Lord, thou knowest it altogether. Thou hast beset me behind and before, and laid thine hand upon me. Such knowledge is too wonderful for me; it is high, I cannot attain unto it."*

The book of Esther is based on revealing the hidden hand of God, who is shifting seasons, reversing the adverse, and revealing a divine design of destiny in the miraculous moments of Biblical feasts.

This is why God in His providence led Esther to unite Purim into the days of destiny known as Biblical feasts.

Esther 9:26-28 tells us, *"Wherefore they called these days Purim after the name of Pur. Therefore for all the words of this letter, and of that which they had seen concerning this matter, and which had come unto them, The Jews ordained, and took upon them, and upon their seed, and upon all such as joined themselves unto them, so as it should not fail, that they would keep these two days according to their writing, and according to their appointed time every year; And that these days should be remembered and kept throughout every generation, every family, every province, and every city; and that these days of Purim should not fail from among the Jews, nor the memorial of them perish from their seed."*

Esther 9:31 continues, *"To confirm these days of Purim in their times appointed, according as Mordecai the Jew and Esther the queen had enjoined them, and as they had decreed for themselves and for their seed, the matters of the fastings and their cry."*

Beloved, thank the Lord for His miraculous moments and for leading us into our days of destiny!

Prayer

Lord, thank You that You are always watching over me, and that Your hand is always guiding me. Thank You for Your personal providence and individual watching in my life! Continue to reveal the plan of destiny that you have for my life, and guide me in your perfect will and timing! In the name of Jesus, amen!

Diary for Destiny

1. Have you ever felt that your heavenly Father does not know about your personal needs? Invite the Lord to reveal His personal providence in your life.

2. How have you seen personal providence and individual watching in your life? Thank the Lord for all that He has done!

3. How have you seen personal providence and individual watching in the lives of others?

Chapter Two

Annihilating Amalek

An Experience In the Megillah Through the Eyes of Esther:

DEADLY DECEPTION

As a little girl, a secret sorrow lay deep in my heart. It was particularly painful when I would see a mother kiss and caress her baby. I would think, "What was *Ima* (Mother) like?" Being bereft of mother and father left me with deep emotions of loneliness lodged in my soul. These are feelings that only an orphan can feel. I felt compelled to connect with my identity and longed to know, "Who am I?" My dear cousin, Mordecai, perceived my pain and understood my dilemma. It was not until he tenderly taught of me about our forefathers and foremothers that I could grasp onto my Hebrew heritage and become closely connected to the pastThe empty ruins in my memory were replaced with lineage (*yichus*) and legacy.

The misplaced and missing pieces of the puzzle began to define my destiny. I am royalty of the house of *Shaul* (Saul), the first king of our people. My cousin Mordecai, the great Torah scholar of our people, captivated my soul by teaching me daily. He lifted my soul by teaching me the concept of *lech lecha*, which means "go to yourself" —your true self and true identity that can only be known through doing Hashem's will. It was in the stillness of those symphonic moments—when sunset transitioned me each day into that holy hour— that my soul was transformed through the words of *Moshe* (Moses) and all of our prophets. The words of fire that birthed forth our nation at Mount Sinai brought my *neshama* (soul) into its highest destiny.

Our family line is connected to Rachel; she is our mother. Cousin Mordecai taught me that, as I studied her greatness, Hashem would infuse into me the same kind of greatness. As our mother, Rachel had given birth to Benjamin, the father of our line. Rachel's first born son, *Yosef* (Joseph), the one sold into slavery, was the *tzadik ha dor* (righteous one) of his generation. Cousin Mordecai taught me that my royal heritage—the line of Rachel, Benjamin, and King Shaul— was my true identity. My cousin also taught me that being the *melech* (king) of *Am Israel* (the people of Israel) meant that Shaul's first and foremost responsibility was to fulfill the command Hashem had given to Joshua and all Israel: "to blot out the remembrance of Amalek from under heaven" (from Deuteronomy 25:19). Amalek is the archenemy of *Am Israel* (the people of Israel).

As the *tzadik ha dor* (righteous one of his generation), my dearest and beloved cousin taught me about certain *middot* (character traits) in our family that needed to be redefined. As descendants of King Shaul, he warned that we, too, could spiral down to a deplorable place if we allowed presumption, pride, and lack of adherence to spiritual authority to enter into our hearts. That was how King Shaul lost his *malchut* (kingship). Cousin Mordecai also taught me that Shaul never completed his mandate to annihilate Amalek.

Our history with Amalek goes back to the days of our patriarchs. The war with Amalek stems from the battle between Jacob and Esau. It is a battle between good and evil that began in the womb. The lifelong intent of Esau was to destroy Jacob. Since the grandson of Esau is Amalek, it grieves me to say that the wicked Haman—who would try to destroy the Jews—is the descendant of Agag, king of the Amalekites. If Shaul had destroyed the Amalekites, Haman would have never risen to power. Instead, Shaul's disobedience affected our people for generations.

My beloved cousin, in his tenderness, considered his greatest responsibility toward me was to raise me in the ways of *derek eretz* (acts of righteousness). I can still hear the whispers of the *Shema,* (the most important prayer of our people), in our house. Early in the morning before the sunrise, Cousin Mordecai would gather all the leaders of Israel, and they would weep for the desolations of Yerushalayim and our Temple. Early in the morning before sunrise, Cousin Mordecai would gather all the leaders

I can still remember how, every evening when I was a child, he would put me on his lap and teach me the Hebrew *aleph beit* (alphabet). He would say, "Come, my little Hadassah, let me teach you the *lashon hakodesh* (holy language) that came from *shamayim* (heaven) to our people." Then, he would give me something sweet to eat and teach me the sweetness of God's holy words. He did this so the *mitzvot* (commandments of our God) would be written on the tablets of my *middot* (character traits).

He would then instill in my heart the legacy of our ancestor, Shaul. I learned from my beloved cousin that, as a daughter in the genealogical line of the royal family, I must be careful to walk and choose a different *derek* (path) than Shaul did. I was made to understand that I could not repeat his character traits, even though I might have had a tendency to do so because of the *yichus* (bloodline). As descendants of Shaul, we needed to guard against the tendency toward disobedience, arrogance, and pride. The disobedience was so strong that it cost my great ancestor his crown (*malchut*). He never fulfilled his destiny to destroy Amalek. Whatever my destiny was, as the descendant of *Shaul HaMelech* (King Saul), I could never achieve it unless those tendencies and character traits were repaired.

Why had Shaul refused to obey *Shmuel HaNavi* (Samuel the prophet) and in destroying the Amalekites? The command to destroy Amalek had been given to our people as a prerequisite to possess the land. As a little child, I had visualized what Amalek had done to our people when we came forth from *Mitzrayim* (Egypt).

Cousin Mordecai taught me that Amalek attacked us in the region near the Red Sea. Hashem blew His *Ruach HaKadosh* (Holy Spirit) and a great wind parted the waves of the mighty waters! During the darkness of the night, Hashem caused a light to go before us as each tribe walked in its own path across dry land in the midst of the sea. The people of Israel crossed safely through the sea to the other side, yet the armies of Pharaoh followed closely behind us. Then came a sudden roar. The wind blew fiercely, and the huge walls of the sea toppled back into their place! Pharaoh and all of his chariots drowned in the sea; all of his horses and riders were swallowed up by the waves of the deep.

Our people camped along the shores of the sea, and as morning came, the rising sun began to glisten upon the sands. Bright rays reflected off the ground in brilliance as the waves brushed over the spoils. On the shores, we could see the chariot wheels made of gold, jewels from the headpieces, and the bracelets of Pharaoh and the Egyptian army. Israel began to glean the shores and carry the spoils into the camp. We had graciously been given jewels of silver and jewels of gold. The booty we collected as a nation from the Red Sea was more than what we had originally brought out of Egypt when we left on the fifteenth of Nisan.

Our God had given us double for our shame. But almost immediately after we harvested the spoils, Amalek attacked us from behind.

We had no water to drink. The Almighty told us that the water was at Mount Sinai, so the elders of our people walked to fetch water from Mount, which was pervading with smoke from the presence of God. Meanwhile, the feeble and lame in the mixed multitude remained behind at Rephidim. Amalek—that vagabond, marauding tribe, which had no fear of God— wanted to lay their hands on the spoil. It was there between the Red Sea and Mount

Sinai—the atmosphere radiating the holiness of God's presence from His mighty wonders in the sea and His majesty upon Mount Sinai—that Amalek attacked our people. Amalek is a physical and spiritual destroyer with only one objective: to destroy Israel.

Knowing the evils of Amalek, I felt within my soul that what my great ancestor, King Shaul, had left unfinished needed to be fulfilled. The crown and the anointing bestowed upon Shaul had been given for the purpose of annihilating Amalek. Could our family line and legacy ever be repaired? Or would the house of my great-ancestor forever be destroyed? A repairing can only be accomplished through finishing what was forfeited. So it was there with my cousin Mordecai—captivated by learning my legacy— that I began to know who I was as a daughter of King Shaul (*bat Shaul*), and understand the calling on my life. Let me teach you the Torah that my cousin Mordecai taught me.

Stepping Stones Into Greatness:

Removing Ourselves from Rephidim (Place of Apathy)

Have you ever blamed yourself for making a deliberate decision that you knew was not the will of God? "If only" are two words that reverberate regret. These two tragic words indicate that there could have been something done to avoid unforeseen circumstances that resulted in various consequences. I once heard Kathryn Kuhlman, the great apostle of the Holy Spirit during the 1970s, say that missing the will of God would be one of the most difficult things a person could experience.

Beloved, I want to make clear that we are limited human beings. Our heavenly Father knows our frame (our *yetzer*, or personality structure), that we are dust. Psalm 103:13-14 says, *"Like as a father pitieth his children, so the Lord pitieth them that fear him. For he knoweth our frame; he remembereth that we are dust."* He knows why we made decisions that may not have been the best choice, or were even completely outside of His perfect will. Dear friends, sometimes these decisions come from disordered emotions, childhood pain, fear, and anxieties, or sometimes we have to make decisions under duress.

Such was the case with the first king of Israel. In 1 Samuel 15, one of the most tragic chapters in the Bible, we see the beginning of long-term consequences for disobedience.

The Bible shows us in 1 Samuel 15 that the prophet Samuel anointed and appointed Saul for the most important military mission any king of Israel would be given. It was not only a command for the national security of Israel, but failure to comply could actually threaten the future of Israel's existence in the land bequeathed to Abraham, Isaac, and Jacob.

We cannot, in any way, compare the calling of Saul and King David. These two kings of the same nation had diverse destinies. As the first king of Israel, Saul was commissioned by commandment to annihilate Amalek, while David was called to destroy the Philistines and establish Jerusalem. The primary purpose of Saul's *meluka* (kingship, from Strong's Hebrew 4410) was to destroy Amalek. As a result of Saul's deliberate disobedience, the seed of Amalek appeared in the person of Haman the Agagite centuries later.

Scripture intends for us to experience the power of Purim in the context of annihilating Amalek. This is why the text goes out of its way to give a brief genealogy of Haman's wicked ancestry. Scripture wants us to understand that the death decree against God's people, written by Haman the son of Hammedatha the Agagite, is a direct connection to Saul's disobedience.

Let us see the magnificent way Scripture connects us to 1 Samuel 15. In Esther 3:1, the text reads, *"After these things did king Ahasuerus promote Haman the son of Hammedatha the Agagite, and advanced him, and set his seat above all the princes that were with him."*

If we remember Biblical history, we know that Agag is the royal title for the Amalekite kings, just as Pharaoh is a generic title for the king of Egypt. In 1 Samuel 15, God instructs Saul to destroy Amalek and everything they had.

As we can see, beloved, Saul's disastrous decision to disobey the most important mandate of his mission cost him his calling. Scripture shows us that the text has deleted him from destiny by blotting out his name from the genealogy. In Esther 2:5, the context concerns itself with ramifications, resulting in the cancellation of his destiny by omitting his name where it should obviously appear. Esther 2:5 says, *"Now in Shushan the palace there was a certain Jew, whose name was Mordecai, the son of Jair, the son of Shimei, the son of Kish, a Benjamite."*

Although Saul had the power and anointing to do exactly what God wanted, he deliberately diverted the command to utterly destroy the Amalekites and kept King Agag alive. 1 Samuel 15:1-3 says, *"Samuel also said unto Saul, The Lord sent me to anoint thee to be king over his people, over Israel: now therefore hearken thou unto the voice of the words of the Lord. Thus saith the Lord of hosts, I remember that which Amalek did to Israel, how he laid wait for him in the way, when he came up from Egypt. Now go and smite Amalek, and utterly destroy all that they have, and spare them not; but slay both man and woman, infant and suckling, ox and sheep, camel and ass."*

1 Samuel 15:7-9 continues, *"And Saul smote the Amalekites from Havilah until thou comest to Shur, that is over against Egypt. And he took Agag the king of the Amalekites alive, and utterly destroyed all the people with the edge of the sword. But Saul and the people spared Agag, and the best of the sheep, and of the oxen, and of the fatlings, and the lambs, and all that was good, and would not utterly destroy them: but every thing that was vile and refuse, that they destroyed utterly."*

We need to understand that there are some intrinsically evil characteristics about Amalek, and there is an ideology about Amalek that needs to be destroyed during Purim. Purim is about spiritually fulfilling God's commandment in Deuteronomy 25:17-19. God wants us to annihilate Amalek in our generation.

Saul's life shows us how partial obedience is considered disobedience to God's will. Saul had been commanded to utterly destroy Amalek, but he only partially obeyed. We see in 1 Samuel 15:8-9 that *"he took Agag the king of the Amalekites alive, and utterly destroyed all the people with the edge of the sword. But Saul and the people spared Agag, and the best of the sheep, and of the oxen, and of the fatlings, and the lambs, and all that was good, and would not utterly destroy them: but every thing that was vile and refuse, that they destroyed utterly."*

When God gives us an order and we have the anointing to do it, we need to obey God in the highest form of excellence and follow His directions exactly. Saul lost the kingdom because he did not follow God's directions, so God gave the throne to David. Notice that David did not inherit the mission of King Saul. David's military mission was to destroy the Philistines and to establish the city of Jerusalem. David was not anointed to destroy the Amalekites. Instead, David was called to destroy the Philistines. The mission of destroying the Amalekites was left undone, since it had been given to Saul.

The book of Exodus shows us that the war with Amalek is an ongoing war. Exodus 17:16 tells us that *"the Lord hath sworn that the Lord will have war with Amalek from generation to generation."* So even though Esther brought down the last of the seed of Agag, we are still at war with the spirit of Amalek. During Purim, God anoints us to wage war with Amalek and drive Amalek out of our ministries, our families, our homes, our finances, and our lives.

In Exodus 17, the text teaches why we must destroy Amalek in every generation. *"And he called the name of the place Massah, and Meribah, because of the chiding of the children of Israel, and because they tempted the Lord, saying, Is the Lord among us, or not? Then came Amalek, and fought with Israel in Rephidim"* (Exodus 17:7-8).

There are several spiritual similitudes that correspond with Israel in Rephidim. The word "Amalek" is numerically equivalent in Hebrew to the word *safek*, which means "doubt." There are times when we may be tempted to doubt our calling, our anointing, our position, and the place where God has put us. We can even begin to doubt everything around us. When we doubt, we open the door to Amalek.

The way that a spirit of Amalek can enter our lives is through doubt. The children of Israel asked, *"Is the Lord*

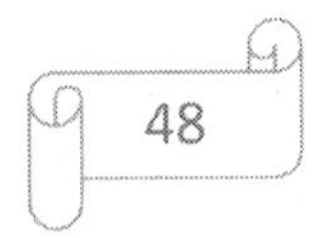

among us, or not?" We may have seen God move miraculously in our lives in the recent past. Perhaps we had a spiritual dream or God gave us a word, but somehow we are now entertaining doubt and we're saying, "Is the Lord among us, or not?"

This is what happened to Israel. They experienced the miracles at the Red Sea and the 10 plagues that brought them out of Egypt. Yet as soon as they began to lack water, they began to doubt.

Let's analyze Exodus 17:7b-8: *"Is the Lord among us, or not? Then came Amalek, and fought with Israel in Rephidim."* Rephidim is a place named by Moses. When the prophets of God named a place or a person, they gave it a name that indicated its spiritual temperature or condition. The given name either characterized a spiritual condition that needed correction, or it indicated a spiritual destiny.

The name "Rephidim" is taken from the root *rapheh* (Strong's Hebrew 7504), which means to weaken, and is related numerically to the word "laxity." Rephidim is a place where Israel's hands were weakened. When we begin to doubt, we open the door to a lethal injection of spiritual apathy.

We can see what happens next in Exodus 17:13-16. "*And Joshua discomfited Amalek and his people with the edge of the sword. And the Lord said unto Moses, Write this for a memorial in a book, and rehearse it in the ears of Joshua: for I will utterly put out the remembrance of Amalek from under heaven. And Moses built an altar, and called the name of it Jehovahnissi: For he said, Because the Lord hath sworn that the Lord will have war with Amalek from generation to generation.*"

What exactly does that mean? We need to understand that after the time of Esther, there were no more Amalekites. So how can God have war with Amalek from generation to generation when there are no more Amalekites on the earth? War continues because Amalek is a spirit and an ideology. Amalek will always be at war with the power and presence of God and the destiny of God's people. Amalek will always be on assignment to destroy the people of God.

We can experience more about why God is insistent on removing the evils of Amalek in the book of Deuteronomy:

Remember what Amalek did unto thee by the way, when ye were come forth out of Egypt; How he met thee by the way, and smote the hindmost of thee, even all that were feeble behind thee, when thou wast faint and weary; and he feared not God. Therefore it shall be, when the Lord thy God hath given thee rest from all thine enemies round about, in the land which the Lord thy God giveth thee for an inheritance to possess it, that thou shalt blot out the remembrance of Amalek from under heaven; thou shalt not forget it (Deuteronomy 25:17-19).

Beloved, remember that every law in the book of Deuteronomy concerns possessing the Promised Land. Deuteronomy teaches us about the possession of promises and inheriting our promised land. That's why God put the commandment about Amalek here again in the book of Deuteronomy, because if we don't destroy Amalek, it means compromising the possession of promises and the inheritance that God is giving us. For Israel, this intrinsic evil cannot be forgotten.

Shabbat Zakor

Shabbat Zakor is the title that refers to the verses of Deuteronomy 25:17-19. In Hebrew, the word *zakor* means "to remember." In Shabbat Zakor, the Almighty is commanding Israel to remember what Amalek did on the way. The command also requires blotting out of the remembrance of Amalek from under heaven. In Deuteronomy 25:19, God commands, *"You shall not forget it."*

Let us see why it is our responsibility to remove the remembrance of Amalek from under heaven. As Deuteronomy 25:17 says, *"Remember what Amalek did unto thee by the way when you were come forth out of Egypt."*

Beloved, this is not a vendetta. This is a commandment to never do to another nation what Amalek did to Israel. Whenever God is giving commandments throughout Torah and He uses the word "remember." The implication is that the Israelites are to remember how it was for them in *Mitzrayim* (Egypt), and never do to others what Mitzrayim did to them.

Applying the hermeneutical method of *gezerah shevah* (equivalence of expressions) to the word "remember" in Scripture are related in meaning and concept. The command to "remember" is specifically applied when referring to the cruel unbearable hardships that *Mitzrayim* (Egypt) used to subjugate Israel. We can see this in the following verses:

"And thou shalt remember that thou wast a bondman in the land of Egypt, and the Lord thy God redeemed thee: therefore I command thee this thing to day" (Deuteronomy 15:15).

"Thou shalt not pervert the judgment of the stranger, nor of the fatherless; nor take a widow's raiment to pledge: But thou shalt remember that thou wast a bondman in Egypt, and the Lord thy God redeemed thee thence: therefore I command thee to do this thing" (Deuteronomy 24:17-18).

"And remember that thou wast a servant in the land of Egypt, and that the Lord thy God brought thee out thence through a mighty hand and by a stretched out arm: therefore the Lord thy God commanded thee to keep the sabbath day" (Deuteronomy 5:15).

When considering these texts, we absolutely know that the God of Abraham, Isaac, and Jacob is all about compassion and mercy; therefore, it cannot be that these commandments in Deuteronomy 25:17-19 (Shabbat Zakor) mean revenge.

We must first understand what Amalek did to the unarmed Israelites coming out of Egypt. In a historical and geographical sense of Scripture, Amalek as a tribe did not have a country. The Amalekites were nomads in the Negev Desert area of Edom. They were an unsettled tribe that made their living by robbing caravans traveling from Mesopotamia to Egypt. As expert robbers, they positioned themselves to lie in wait when Israel came out of Egypt.

Specifically, the text teaches in Exodus 17:5-6, *"And the Lord said unto Moses, Go on before the people, and take with thee of the elders of Israel; and thy rod, wherewith thou smotest the river, take in thine hand, and go. Behold, I will stand before thee there upon the rock in Horeb; and thou shalt smite the rock, and there shall come water out of it, that the people may drink. And Moses did so in the sight of the elders of Israel."*

God told Moses to go with the elders of Israel to get the water at Mount Horeb (Mount Sinai). Geographically, the location was within walking distance from Rephidim. When the others in the camp heard the gushing water flooding out of the rock, they ran to the water to quench their thirst. The weak and the feeble lagged behind with no protection, completely unarmed. This is when the Amalekites made their cruel, vicious attack. Their attack aimed to rob the camp of the substance they had brought out of Egypt. This outrage by heaven demonstrates how God feels when His beloved children are plundered of their inheritance. Amalek *"feared not God"* (Deuteronomy 25:18b). There was no fear of the God who had parted the Red Sea and had done mighty works for Israel. In a brazen rejection of divine intervention, Amalek disregards these acts of God. Instead of seeing providence, Amalek calls them coincidence. This is seen in Deuteronomy 25:18a, which says *"How he met thee by the way."* In Hebrew, this phrase is *Asher karkah ba derek*.

Let's take a closer look at the components of this verse. When we look at the word *karkah*, we see that the Hebrew letters *kuf* and *reish* in the prefix of *karkah* translate to the word "cold." This phrase can, therefore, be rendered as "Amalek cooled us off." Through the doubt and the apathy at Rephidim, Israel became dangerously vulnerable to the door of deception through Amalek.

The word *karkah* is also related in Hebrew to the word *mikreh* (Strong's Hebrew 4745) and *qareh* (Strong's Hebrew 7137), which both mean "chance." Therefore, Deuteronomy 25:18a can also be read as "How he chanced upon thee by the way." This "chancing" describes the concept of coincidence. The concept of coincidence denies the divine interaction of God in the lives of His dear children. It tries to give a logical explanation for the miraculous hidden hand of God. It says that any surprise meetings or circumstances are simply coincidence.

This ideology of coincidence, rather than belief in the supernatural setups of divine providence, is quite contrary to the teaching of the Bible. This ideology of coincidence rather than providence is seen throughout the Scripture when encountering Amalek.

For example, we see in 2 Samuel 1 how an Amalekite considered it chance to fall upon King Saul when he was wounded in the battle. 2 Samuel 1:6-8 says, *"And the young man that told him said, As I happened by chance upon mount Gilboa, behold, Saul leaned upon his spear; and, lo, the chariots and horsemen followed hard after him. And when he looked behind him, he saw me, and called unto me. And I answered, Here am I. And he said unto me, Who art thou? And I answered him, I am an Amalekite."*

This understanding of Amalek is a critical key in understanding how Haman cast *pur* in Esther 3:7 to see by chance what would be the most advantageous day to destroy the Jews. Esther 3:7 says, *"In the first month, that is, the month Nisan, in the twelfth year of king Ahasuerus, they cast Pur, that is, the lot, before Haman from day to day, and from month to month, to the twelfth month, that is, the month Adar."*

The Door to Deception, Apathy, and Amalek: Better Beware of the Complacency Complex

Haman was able to gain power because the children of Israel were in the spiritual condition of Rephidim again. In Esther 1, the children of Israel who lived in Persia were in a state of spiritual apathy because they were in a place of complacency. They should have already responded to the Lord and returned to the Promised Land to rebuild the Temple. Jeremiah 29:10 says, *"For thus saith the Lord, That after seventy years be accomplished at Babylon I will visit you, and perform my good word toward you, in causing you to return to this place."*

One hundred and seventy five years before Cyrus was born, Isaiah prophesied that he would be the chosen vessel to break the bondage of the Babylonian captivity (see Isaiah 45:1-3). The fulfillment of Isaiah's prophecy and Jeremiah's prophecy were manifested in Ezra 1:1-3, which says, *"Now in the first year of Cyrus king of Persia, that the word of the Lord by the mouth of Jeremiah might be fulfilled, the Lord stirred up the spirit of Cyrus king of*

Persia, that he made a proclamation throughout all his kingdom, and put it also in writing, saying, Thus saith Cyrus king of Persia, The Lord God of heaven hath given me all the kingdoms of the earth; and he hath charged me to build him an house at Jerusalem, which is in Judah. Who is there among you of all his people? his God be with him, and let him go up to Jerusalem, which is in Judah, and build the house of the Lord God of Israel, (he is the God,) which is in Jerusalem."

Cyrus had made a proclamation of emancipation that the people of God could return to the Promised Land and rebuild the Temple, and that he would even finance the project, but the children of Israel were too content with their captivity to fulfill the will of God.

But God already had His plan in place before the evil plot described in Esther 3:7 developed. Although Haman was chancing upon Israel with coincidence, God immediately reversed it to providence. God wants you to know that whatever the enemy has planned to destroy you, God will use it to deploy you into His highest purpose.

Notice how quickly the supernatural shift or reversal takes place through the double entendre of Esther 3:7. A double entendre is a word or phrase with two interpretations. Esther 3:7 says, *"In the first month, that is, the month Nisan, in the twelfth year of king Ahasuerus, they cast Pur, that is, the lot, before Haman from day to day, and from month to month, to the twelfth month, that is, the month Adar." "In the first month, that is, the month Nisan"* is a double entendre. Nisan (Nes) means "miracles" and is the month of redemption out of Egypt.

"They cast pur, that is, the lot" is another double entendre. From a hermeneutical standpoint, the prophetic agenda and the author's intent was to differentiate a division between the two meanings of casting pur and casting lots by using the literary device of the double entendre.

From a Biblical perspective, casting pur is a form of chance, coincidence, and superstition. The casting of lots is a form of *hashgacha pratis* (divine providence). The casting of lots is used throughout the Bible whenever Israel needed a divine decision too important for Israel to make without God.

God calls the shots. He makes the divine decisions over your life. He has ordered our steps in His Word. Psalm 37:23 says, *"The steps of a good man are ordered by the Lord: and he delighteth in his way,"* and Psalm 119:133 tells us, *"Order my steps in thy word: and let not any iniquity have dominion over me."* God wants us to know that He is the God who will turn any mistake into a miracle. He can take any plot and turn it into a plan for good. Before the pur ever hit the ground, as ordered by the wicked Haman, God already changed it. He called it the lot (*goral*), not pur. This means it's not Haman's decision; it is God's decision. As Proverbs 16:33 (NIV) says, *"The lot is cast into the lap, but its every decision is from the Lord."*

The casting of lots as a form of *hashgacha pratis* (divine providence or divine decision) is used 70 times in the Hebrew Scriptures. The closest connection with casting lots is in Joshua, Chapters 14-21. Joshua 18:6 tells us, *"Ye shall therefore describe the land into seven parts, and bring the description hither to me, that I may cast lots for you here before the Lord our God."*

Beloved, God will always demonstrate His divine providence and reverse the adverse in our lives!

Prayer

Lord, deliver us from the robbing spirit of Amalek! Let us never be lukewarm, but let us always be on fire for You! Forgive us for not giving You the glory in every situation in our lives. Open our eyes to see Your divine providence and direction in every area of our lives. In the name of Jesus, amen!

Diary for Destiny

1. What is God's will for your life? Just as Saul was called to annihilate Amalek, and David was called to destroy the Philistines and establish Jerusalem, God has a purpose and a plan for your life! Invite the Lord to further reveal His calling and destiny for you.

2. Has God given you certain instructions to do something, but you have either disobeyed or partially obeyed Him? Ask the Lord for forgiveness, and ask Him to give you the strength and determination to carry out the tasks.

Chapter Three

The Diadem of Destiny

An Experience In the Megillah Through the Eyes of Esther:

THE ATTRIBUTES of GREATNESS

Every woman throughout the empire experienced the fall of Vashti. It caused life as we knew it to be drastically changed. A tremendous sense of social pressure arose. Not only was a *dat* (decree) written that removed Vashti from her position and initiated a search for a new queen, but it also commanded that all women, regardless of status, to never react boldly or independently outside of the wishes of their husbands or of any male member in their nearest of kin. All women were suddenly and sharply confined under an oppressive demand of compliance and servitude. As a result of Vashti's behavior, the *dat* (decree) caused a devastating effect that changed the lives of all women in the empire forever. Failure to obey this dat could result in an end like that of Vashti. This fear restricted our freedom and forced us to comply as members of a secondary class of citizens. All of our honor and dignity were stripped from us. The search for a new queen had additional, dire consequences for those of us in the empire who were young women, and also for our families. As the search began, young women were taken by force from village to village to Shushan the palace. Echoes in the wind resounded with the screams and cries from the fairest and most beautiful of our daughters. Our fathers and mothers plunged to the ground, crying out for mercy. I could hear Rachel weeping for her children, who refused to be comforted because her daughters were being stolen away and she would see them no more.

Our daughters were taken as a part of a dreadful deportation. This deportation was unlike before, with chains and whips as in Egypt. This time, it happened with caravans covered in silk, and dromedaries laden with silver and gold. I can remember our fathers pleading in various languages. Some of our brothers came forward, offering themselves as slaves in exchange for their sisters' freedom. All the young, beautiful virgins throughout the entire 127 provinces of the empire, from the largest cities to the smallest villages, could be taken from their homes to be placed in the house of women at Shushan the palace—never to return or ever see their families again.

On that devastating day when the captors came to take me, the outcome was inevitable, but still, my cousin pleaded in desperation for my release by offering everything we owned in exchange. He promised to work for the rest of his life to translate their writings into Hebrew if only they would not force me to be taken to the house of women. The captors had almost been persuaded by the irresistible offer when suddenly the words, "That one, bring me that one," resounded in my ears. At that moment I knew my life would be changed forever. My heart plunged within me and my blood began racing. My cousin then cried out in desperation in one final plea, "I will pay you five shekels of silver if you will just allow me to place a special *brachah* (blessing) upon her from our God!"

The king's chamberlain, carried on a bed, clapped his hands and demanded that his servants feed him bread and grapes. Time stopped ticking. A heavenly pause was granted. Divine providence arranged that a *brachah* (blessing) be pronounced over me before I was taken.

My cousin hastened as he reverently girded himself with his *tallit* (prayer shawl). He lifted the holy corners to his lips and kissed the corners as was his custom. His tallit was so precious to him as it represented all of God's commandments. As he stretched out his hand toward my head to pray for me, I could smell the leather strap of

his *tefillin* (phylactery) wrapped between his fingers and forearm.
As my cousin pronounced the brachah, his gentle strong voice cracked as his petition entered *shamayim* (heaven). "Blessed are You, O Lord, King of the Universe. You have entrusted Your daughter Hadassah into my care. Just as Joseph our ancestor through Rachel our mother was taken down into Mitzrayim and emerged into greatness, bring forth Your daughter into her destiny for such a time as this."

I could feel the warm tears trickle down his face as he tenderly entrusted me into the hands of the Almighty. A peace calmed my whimpering soul as I was ushered into a presence that felt like a father holding his precious daughter. It was my heavenly Father responding to the *tefillah* (prayer) of my cousin.

Then my cousin whispered, "Hadassah, listen to my voice, my child. Things are beginning to change in the empire. I am hearing reports that are coming from Yerushalayim that are affecting the way people perceive the Jews. I sense something very dark is coming upon us. It makes this moment of parting almost unbearable."

"Listen, my child," he continued, breathing heavily as if a weight had dropped upon him. "Tell no one you are a Jew. I know this, my child, from the *Ruach HaKadosh*

(Holy Spirit). The people in the palace must think of you as a *goy* (Gentile). Something is urging me. We must change your name. Surely they will know you are a Jew if you keep the name Hadassah. Fear no man. Hashem is with you. My little Hadassah, your new name will reveal this mission Hashem is giving you. With this name you must remember to hide yourself and your people. Your new name shall be called Esther. Whenever it is spoken, it will remind you of this command that I gave you this day, my child. Let no one know you are a Jew."

"Beloved cousin, everything is taken from me this day – my home, you, and my people!" I began to sob. Suddenly, overnight everything was taken: my home, my cousin, and now my identity.

His deep brown eyes filled with fiery wisdom and gazed upon me for a splendid second. Then he said in gentle strength, "Did not our forefather Abraham come into greatness by leaving his land, his father's house, and his people? Did not our mother Sarah also separate from her kindred people to go to a land that our God would reveal to them?"

He then wrapped me in my favorite multicolored garment, rushing me along since we could hear the sounds of the servants loading the caravan beginning to fade. "Go, my Hadassah – become Esther. Go to yourself (*lech lecha*), my beloved child. Hashem shall honor us. He shall provide a way that I can send you secret messages. He will be with you. He will give you a special sign from *shamayim* (heaven)." Our moment together came to an end, and I was commanded into the caravan. My heart pounded and again I felt the familiar empty isolation of the past from losing my parents. As we moved along, I heard the echoes in my mind: "Do not tell them you are a Jew. Your name will be Esther."

As we approached Shushan the palace, the clanking of the caravan began to sound slower and soon came to a halt. I took off my shawl to cover some of the younger girls who had fallen asleep. The one in front of me looked so familiar. I recalled seeing her in the marketplace before Shabbat. Little did I know then that we would be in the same place right now.

I could hardly sleep the first night in Shushan the palace. Flashes of being taken and Cousin Mordecai pleading for me continued in my mind throughout the night. Then, suddenly I heard whimpers across the room where I had been placed in the house of women. I walked over to the place where several girls were lying on carpets. A girl a bit younger than myself was crying and crying. As I beheld her puffy little wet face, I saw another just like her. I took them both and began to rock them, realizing I

would now give back the *chesed* (loving-kindness) that Cousin Mordecai had given to me.
With Hashem's help, I began to see this place differently. There were so many needs. Perhaps Hashem had a plan for me here. I would try to be the mother that these girls had now lost. Hadassah the orphan would become Esther a mother to those whom I so identified with. Compelled by compassion, I no longer felt like Hadassah the orphan.

Early in the morning, we embarked upon our training. A kind but strict voice became as a shrill calling us to the table. After our meal, we began learning about the king, the government, and the culture of this land. This became our daily routine. I became well educated in the Achaemenid Empire.

The chamberlain over our training, a man known as Hege, began to see that my values and my life reflected a different perspective than the others. He would say, "Esther, you are not of this world." I came into great favor with him. Like Joseph of old (my beloved ancestor) and like Daniel, I was placed above all who were before me by the chamberlain. He gave me a preferred position.

Even with all the position and title I had been given in the house of women, the only thing I wanted to do was be pleasing to the King of heaven who was now my closest companion. Let me tell you why pleasing the King is the only thing I desire.

Stepping Stones Into Greatness:

Character Traits God Uses

and

Character Traits God Refuses

You may ask the question, "What does it take to come into a place of greatness?" God told Abram in Genesis 12:2a, *"And I will make of thee a great nation, and I will make thy name great."*

From the beginning, God's call to Abram was to be the father of a great nation and of a people of greatness. The life of Abraham was to be a reflection of the perfection of the greatness that would define the destiny of his descendants.

Greatness is the primary requirement on the resume of destiny throughout the Bible. God told Jacob how the people destined for greatness would attain it. Genesis 46:3 says, *"And he said, I am God, the God of thy father: fear not to go down into Egypt; for I will there make of thee a great nation."*

God did not form His people into the greatness destined for them in the land of Canaan. God formed them into a people of greatness in Egypt. It was not God's plan to make a people of greatness in the land of Canaan. Canaan was their inheritance. It was in the crucible of testing in the fiery furnace of Egypt that God made the people of greatness.

What does it mean to be a people of greatness? Greatness is the emergence of character traits that become the stepping stones into destiny. Every person in the Bible that attained the highest dimension of destiny that God ordained for them attained greatness of character.

In the book of Esther, Scripture introduces us to Esther and Mordecai with the intention of revealing their greatness in the sight of God in terms of their character. These attributes of greatness will become the qualification for exaltation into destiny. We see the concept of greatness emphasized throughout the book of Esther. The book of Esther begins with emphasizing Mordecai's connection to the tribe of Judah, the kingly tribe of Israel, and ends with describing Mordecai's greatness. As Esther 10:3 says, *"For Mordecai the Jew was next to King Ahasuerus and great among the Jews, and accepted of the multitude of his brethren, seeking the wealth of his people, and speaking peace to all his seed."*

This emphasis on greatness appears early in the book of Esther in what seems to be a double identity when Mordecai is introduced to us. This concept of a double identity will be woven into the genealogy and backdrop of both Esther and Mordecai.

Esther 2:5 says, *"Now in Shushan the palace, there was a certain Jew [Yehudi], whose name was Mordecai, the son of Jair, the son of Shimei, the son of Kish, a Benjamite."* In a genealogical sense of Scripture, Mordecai is Ben-Yemeni, a Benjamite, but he is also called Yehudi, from the tribe of Judah, in another sense. The question arises, "Why does the *megillah* (scroll) present two identities?"

We know that Mordecai is definitely Ben-Yemeni from this *yichus* (lineage). In an intercontextual sense of Scripture, the text is also drawing a connection between Mordecai and the tribe of Judah, the kingly tribe of Israel, based on the greatness of Mordecai's character.

The resolution to the apparent problem of Mordecai being identified as both Ben-Yemeni and Yehudi is that the context connects Mordecai to Yehudi (Judah) through a reference to King David. This is done in the irregular genealogy that traces the ancestry of Mordecai to Shimei (Esther 2:5). Why Shimei? The peculiar position of Shimei in the genealogy of Mordecai brings discord in the continuity. Historically, Shimei is one of the most contemptible individuals in the line of Benjamin. Shimei's name is known because of his despicable behavior toward King David. His unkind, cruel, disrespectful behavior toward David is elaborated upon in 2 Samuel 16, only to teach us the greatness of King David's response toward him.

2 Samuel 16:5-13 says, *"And when king David came to Bahurim, behold, thence came out a man of the family of the house of Saul, whose name was Shimei, the son of Gera: he came forth, and cursed still as he came. And he cast stones at David, and at all the servants of king David: and all the people and all the mighty men were on his right hand and on his left. And thus said Shimei when he cursed, Come out, come out, thou bloody man, and thou man of Belial: The Lord hath returned upon thee all the blood of the house of Saul, in whose stead thou hast reigned; and the Lord hath delivered the kingdom into the hand of Absalom thy son: and, behold, thou art taken in thy mischief, because thou art a bloody man. Then said*

Abishai the son of Zeruiah unto the king, Why should this dead dog curse my lord the king? let me go over, I pray thee, and take off his head. And the king said, What have I to do with you, ye sons of Zeruiah? so let him curse, because the Lord hath said unto him, Curse David. Who shall then say, Wherefore hast thou done so? And David said to Abishai, and to all his servants, Behold, my son, which came forth of my bowels, seeketh my life: how much more now may this Benjamite do it? let him alone, and let him curse; for the Lord hath bidden him. ***It may be that the Lord will look on mine affliction, and that the Lord will requite me good for his cursing this day.*** *And as David and his men went by the way, Shimei went along on the hill's side over against him, and cursed as he went, and threw stones at him, and cast dust."*

The concept of greatness is such an essential element for destiny that Scripture includes it as a theme when presenting the genealogies of Mordecai and Esther. In 2 Samuel 16, the valiant reaction of King David in his refusal to entertain revenge, even in justifiable circumstances, becomes part of Mordecai's legacy through Shimei. By adding Shimei to the genealogy of Mordecai, Scripture heralds the heroic character traits that teach us about greatness through the incident of King David and Shimei. If King David had responded in revenge by not letting Shimei live, Mordecai would not have been born.

Taking Responsibility

We all have a deep desire hidden in our hearts for destiny. How do we define destiny? You may ask the question, "How do I achieve the highest predestined purpose in my life?" Do we achieve it by success strategies? Is devising a carefully calculated plan the stepping stone into the dream? Of course preparing a plan to reach our goals is definitely one of the greatest Biblical success secrets. Esther prepared the plan given to her by God during her three days of prayer and fasting (Esther 4:16).

Similarly, in the life of King David, Scripture shows us the importance of having a plan in the way that he prepared the plan for Solomon's Temple before he went to heaven. 1 Chronicles 22:5 says, "*And David said, Solomon my son is young and tender, and the house that is to be builded for the Lord must be exceeding magnifical, of fame and of glory throughout all countries: I will therefore now make preparation for it. So David prepared abundantly before his death.*" 1 Chronicles 28:11-12 continues, "*Then David gave to Solomon his son the pattern of the porch, and of the houses thereof, and of the treasuries thereof, and of the upper chambers thereof, and of the inner parlours thereof, and of the place of the mercy seat, And the pattern of all that he had by the spirit, of the courts of the house of the Lord, and of all the chambers round about, of the treasuries of the house of God, and of the treasuries of the dedicated things."*

This text teaches that visions and dreams metamorphose from thoughts to reality by the power of a plan. We see further evidence of the power of having a plan in Joshua 7 and 8, which shows us that the only casualty in the career of Joshua in the mandate to conquer Canaan happened when there was not a plan. Although having a plan is one of the most essential elements in achieving our goals, it is not the core cause of what determines destiny in our lives. Throughout the Bible, there is a consistency and a continuity that reveals the greatest success secret above all others. This success secret is the quality of our character.

Whenever the Bible credentials the call into greatness, it always presents the character trait test. The character trait test is a procedure that ascertains proof of an individual's intentions and purposes. In the book of 1 Samuel, Chapters 16-30 deal with David's response to the malicious, hostile, contentious, cruel, and competitive attacks from Saul his father-in-law. His responses to these difficult tests were the determining dynamic of his destiny.

The quality of our character in light of the circumstances and the duress that we encounter determines our success. In 1 Samuel 16-30, the Bible documents the details of the severities and sufferings in David's soul for 15 chapters, because it recognizes his response as the most critical component for the diadem of destiny in his life.

Let us look at how Scripture similarly presents the attributes of greatness in Mordecai. In Esther 2:5-7, the context concerns itself with the outstanding character traits and attributes of greatness in Mordecai.

Esther 2:5-7 says, *"Now in Shushan the palace there was a certain Jew, whose name was Mordecai, the son of Jair, the son of Shimei, the son of Kish, a Benjamite; Who had been carried away from Jerusalem with the captivity which had been carried away with Jeconiah king of Judah, whom Nebuchadnezzar the king of Babylon had carried away. And he brought up Hadassah, that is, Esther, his uncle's daughter: for she had neither father nor mother, and the maid was fair and beautiful; whom Mordecai, when her father and mother were dead, took for his own daughter."*

Notice, beloved, the systematic order of the text. In a hermeneutical sense of Scripture, the composition is written so that the identity of Mordecai is not isolated from his outstanding and praiseworthy character traits (*middot*). We saw earlier how the genealogy of Mordecai shows how he is linked to King David, who demonstrated great kindness when he refused to let Shimei, Mordecai's ancestor, be killed, even though Shimei had cursed him. The text is implying that Mordecai and Esther are preserved in posterity because of the noble character traits of King David.

We see further evidence of Mordecai's character in the texts that follow. Let's take a look at Esther 2:7, which says, *"And he brought up Hadassah, that is, Esther, his uncle's daughter: for she had neither father nor mother, and the maid was fair and beautiful; whom Mordecai, when her mother and father were dead, took for his own daughter."* Scripture twice repeats that Esther had no father and mother, and that Mordecai brought her up and took her for his own daughter. The Bible is emphasizing that Mordecai took responsibility for Esther, which is one of the most important character traits in Scripture that qualifies an individual for the platform of predestined purpose and greatness.

What does it mean to take responsibility for another person, and how does that qualify us for the platform of purpose and destiny? Scripture prizes taking responsibility for another as a prerequisite for qualified leadership.

In the book of Genesis, several years after Joseph had been sold as a slave by his brothers, famine was raging in the land of Canaan. Wheat was running out. Water was scarce. The sons of Jacob were in a dangerous plight. The only place to buy food was Egypt.

The sons of Jacob had no idea that the viceroy who was managing distribution of food for the nations was their brother Joseph. When they came to Egypt seeking bread, Joseph required that in order to be sustained by the abundant supply in Egypt, they needed to bring back their youngest brother Benjamin to prove the sincerity of their story. When the sons of Jacob returned to their father, his reluctance and fear to let Benjamin return with his brethren was something he refused to do based on his constant grief and sorrow in believing that Joseph, Benjamin's older brother and son of his beloved Rachel, was dead.

Jacob did not want to lose another son. His soul was bound up in Benjamin because he represented his only tangible connection to Rachel and Joseph. Asking Jacob to release Benjamin to go down to Egypt was more than he could bear. To Jacob, it triggered the possible tragedy of loss that he could not bear in his old age.

Suddenly, Judah stepped up to the plate, and gave his father assurance by his willingness to take responsibility. Genesis 43:8-9 says, *"And Judah said unto Israel his father, Send the lad with me, and we will arise and go; that we may live, and not die, both we, and thou, and also our little ones; I will be surety for him; of my hand shalt thou require him: if I bring him not unto thee, and set him before thee, then let me bear the blame for ever."* This noble, courageous, unselfish act of being willing to take the responsibility that he would bear the blame in order to spare others is a character trait that passed from Judah to his descendants.

This character trait is worthy of the diadem of destiny. Judah's excellent, extraordinary character calmed the fears of the aged Jacob, who was still traumatized from the two losses of those he loved the most. The sudden sorrow of Rachel's premature death and the unresolved issues of Jacob's bloody coat would have made it impossible for Jacob to release Benjamin if it were not for Judah. This is why Jacob pronounced a destiny blessing for Judah, saying, *"The scepter shall not depart from Judah"* (Genesis 49:10a).

Likewise, in Esther 2:7, we see the qualification of exaltation into destiny by Mordecai's acts of tenderness and care for Esther. He not only takes responsibility for her, but Scripture shows us the added element of *chesed* (loving-kindness) and compassion. Esther 2:7 says,

"When her mother and father were dead, he looked on her as his own daughter."

"He looked on her as his own daughter" means that Mordecai loved Esther with an added element of tender compassion and love that was more than just fulfilling his duty. There is a compassion conveyed in the context which shows that the sense of isolation and abandonment felt in the heart of Esther was satiated by Mordecai's fatherly care.

The text continues to elucidate the concept of character traits. Esther was fully aware of the rebellious tendencies of her ancestor Saul, and the submissive, humble character of Esther was put to the test. But even behind closed doors, never seeing Mordecai's face, Esther remained consistent in her commitment to obey Mordecai. Esther 2:10 tells us, *"Esther had not shewed her people nor her kindred: for Mordecai had charged her that she should not shew it."*

Esther's personality profile demonstrates the quality of *menuchat ha nefesh* (equanimity), which means that her character traits were not affected in a negative sense by difficult or challenging circumstances.

The portrait of her inner beauty is also described through the character trait of *tzinuit* (modesty). Tzinuit is not just outward modesty. Someone can dress very modestly but still constantly draw attention to themselves and their own behavior in word and deed.

Tzinuit is a quality that is so precious to God that it was the determining dynamic that led Saul to be chosen as the first king of Israel. 1 Samuel 15:17 says, *"And Samuel said, When thou wast little in thine own sight, wast thou not made the head of the tribes of Israel, and the Lord anointed thee king over Israel?"*

Esther brought back the qualities of *menuchat ha nefesh* and *tzinuit* to the royal bloodline of Saul. As Esther 2:20 tells us, *"Esther had not yet shewed her kindred nor her people; as Mordecai had charged her: for Esther did the commandment of Mordecai, like as when she was brought up with him."*

Beloved, just like Mordecai and Esther, let our characters be refined so that we are qualified for greatness!

Prayer

Lord God, I ask you to develop character traits in me that are worthy of the diadem of destiny. I want to experience what both Mordecai and Esther experienced. Strengthen my character, and help me to take responsibility for others. In the name of Jesus, amen!

Diary for Destiny

1. Taking responsibility for another person is one of the most important character traits in Scripture. Who have you taken responsibility for in the past? Who are you currently taking responsibility for?

2. What are your strongest character qualities? What areas of your character need to be strengthened? Ask the Lord right now to improve these areas of your character so that you are qualified for greatness!

Chapter Four

Disannulling the Decree

An Experience In the Megillah Through the Eyes of Esther:

Reverse the Adverse

One day, during a time when I was older, the entire city of Shushan erupted into a condition of chaos. The great King Ahasuerus, son of Cyrus the Great, hosted a feast and invited everyone—both great and small, with or without pedigree —to his palace. Those who were not normally allowed to approach his gates were now eating and drinking in his courts. It was there on the seventh day of the feast that I first learned of the *dat* (decree) and its devastating rule over the empire. In some kingdoms, the word of the king was its highest authority, but in the Achaemenid empire of the Medes and the Persians, the dat was of a higher authority than even the gods they worshipped. No man could reverse a royal decree, not even the king.

My beloved cousin Mordecai, whom I refer to as Mordecai the Great out of respect for his position, was a dignified statesman who also attended the feast. Mordecai attended only out of protocol for his position as an elder among the king's servants, and warned me that we should stay kosher and never involve ourselves in the practices of the *goyim* (Gentiles). Practicing a kosher lifestyle in a meticulous manner was especially important for my beloved cousin Mordecai, who was the *tzadik ha dor* (righteous man of his generation).

Suddenly, silence swept across the feast as the king's chamberlains invaded the banquet of women, and demanded that the queen, Vashti, appear before the king. The captivating, beautiful Queen Vashti was called to come into the banquet of men. How could it be that the great granddaughter of King Nebuchadnezzar was being made to stoop to such a menial status? How could she be called in front of men in their drunken condition? Her brazen refusal demonstrated her disgust towards such a vile command. It was known that King Ahasuerus was not of the same pedigree as the great Queen Vashti. However, no one had ever refused the command of the king; such an action was not allowed among the Medes and the Persians.

In a frenzied fury, King Ahasuerus called his chamberlains to immediately deliberate actions toward Queen Vashti. Then that evil Memuchan (also known as Haman) advised the king that one person's behavior could affect everyone else in the empire. In his typical manner, he connived and convinced the king that a royal edict and irreversible decree should immediately be devised against Vashti the queen. Therefore, it was decreed under royal edict that could not be altered or reversed that Vashti the queen come no more into the presence of the king, and that her royal estate be given to another that was better than she. This tyrannical decree was perpetrated against the women to intimidate us to never speak, but most of all to teach us to fear the *dat* (decree).

But while this particular dat had terrible repercussions for Vashti and the women of the Medean-Persian empire, little did I know that a dat even more diabolical would soon be written against *Am Israel* (the people of Israel)!

Let me tell you how it all began. During my captivity, while I was in the house of women, the time of preparation to go before the king lasted a year. Hege spent many long hours training us in the house of women to be pleasing to the king. But I came to realize that my true king was the King of heaven. I lived only for Him and for His sake.

I knew in the depths of my being that my only king was Hashem. How could I ever recognize anyone else as a king but Him? The kingdom of King Ahasuerus was ruled under the dominion of the dat. My King, the *Melech* of the Universe, gave His subjects commandments that lift us up to our highest destiny. How hard it was for me to understand a kingdom ruled by the dat and its foolish laws. The King of heaven rules His subjects with his Torah and His *mitzvot* (commandments) that raise us up high above all the people of the earth.

As Hege spent long painstaking hours instructing us, my heart was constantly lifted to my true King. I wanted all my thoughts, desires, and actions to please only Him. Although I was locked away in a place where I did not want to be, I showed *chesed* (loving-kindness) in every way that I could to those around me.

I remember one day in particular that is forever etched and impressed in the chambers of my memory. It happened on a day when we were under Hege's special guidance and tutoring before we had our individual time with the king. Hege thought it would be expedient for us to practice our walk from the house of women to the king's court. We disembarked outside from the house of women. With veiled faces, and surrounded by the king's guards, we began our training for the walk that we would each encounter when it was our time to be with the king. Hege wanted us to be familiar with the way that the path looked at night, for it was customary that we would be called at night.

Around sunset on the day that we were practicing the walk, as the brilliant rays came down like gold over the courtyard, the thoughts of my heart were no longer in Persia. The golden sunsets amidst the walls of Shushan were a constant reminder of our holy city, Yerushalayim, which lay in desolation and destruction from the dreadful day of *Tish B'Av*. With my heart uplifted to my God in the silence of my heart, I offered a *tefillah* (prayer) in the hiddenness of my soul for *Shivat Zion* (return to Zion).

My thoughts were abruptly interrupted by the sound of a demanding, cruel voice that I heard off in the distance. As we walked through the courtyard, amidst the sounds of horses and trumpets, a voice proclaimed, "All servants who reside within the king's gate are commanded to be under the authority of Memuchan (Haman)!"

For a moment, as I glanced upward when I beheld this man, it was as if all others around him were covered in dark shadows. I could see only him. No one else seemed visible. As I gazed, it was as if my soul was suspended in time. Who was this man who became the only one that I could see while the others were hidden in the shadows?

The darkness around this man became more apparent to me as I continued to watch his boisterous demeanor, and I felt chills rise through my body. Terror seemed to strike me. The glorious experience I had in prayer a few moments earlier, recalling the desolation of the holy city, seemed to have ceased with this unwelcome intrusion. The more that I stared at this man, fear and anxiety crept in my heart. I could hear the echoes of his brutal behavior toward those who gathered around the king's gate. This seemed so inappropriate since they also were the king's servants and men of dignity. As he spoke to them, I felt an alarm. Then suddenly, I looked upon his robes and very visibly I could see the symbol of the tribe of Amalek. It was a royal symbol, the symbol of King Agag of the Amalekites. I understood, then, that the man they referred to as "Memuchan" was also known as "Haman," of the seed of Agag, king of the Amalekites.

Let me tell you how our people rose up against this Memuchan (Haman) and his *dat* (decree) through prayer and fasting. I will speak of how my God turned the irreversible decree for His people. If my God did it for *Am Israel* (the people of Israel), He will also do it for you.

Stepping Stones Into Greatness:

How to Disannul the Decree in Your Life

One of the most intriguing critical components in the book of Esther is found in the concept and word "decree." It was a decree that almost destroyed six million Jews living in the Persian Empire during the time of King Ahasuerus in the twelfth year of his reign in the year 473 B.C. We may ask the question, "How can one decree have such an effect in a kingdom that it mandates the extermination of six million of its faithful subjects?"

A key element in understanding how Haman's decree had such power over the Jewish people is to first understand the concept of the decree in light of Medean-Persian history.

In a literary sense of Scripture, the word "decree" is used in the original Hebrew language 19 times in *Megillah Esther* (the scroll, or book, of Esther). The unusual employment of the word "decree" was used specifically by Esther and Mordecai as a unique literary device, known as the *millah min ha ah* (guiding word). This literary tool was used to cohere the text together in a thematic unity. The *millah min ha ah* (guiding word) presents the author's intent to display the decree as a primary theme in the miraculous deliverance that God brought to His people.

Definition of "Decree" in the Medean-Persian Culture

So what is a decree, and what is the historical relevance of the word "decree"?

The word "decree" when translated from English to Hebrew is the word *dat*. Dat is not originally a Hebrew word but is a Persian derivative used specifically in *Megillah Esther* (the scroll or book of Esther), *Sefer Daniel* (the book of Daniel), and *Sefer Ezra* (the book of Ezra). This word has its own autonomous meaning in the books of Esther, Daniel, and Ezra.

In Biblical times, most civilizations and empires outside the land of Israel considered their emperors to be the supreme deity in their pantheon of gods. In the Medean-Persian Empire, there was one entity greater than the emperor. This was the royal decree called the *dat*. Once a dat was signed by the emperor with his royal seal after the scribes had drafted it, it could never be reversed or altered. This meant that all levels of Persian society submitted themselves to the rule of the dat. The *dat* (royal decree) had more political power and influence than the word of the king. Even the king could not reverse or alter the dat.

In *Sefer Daniel* (the book of Daniel), the text teaches how King Darius greatly desired to deliver Daniel from the den of lions by reversing the dat, but it could not be changed under the laws of the Medes and Persians. Daniel 6:8-10,12 says, *"Now, O king, establish the decree, and sign the writing, that it be not changed, according to the law of the Medes and Persians, which altereth not. Wherefore king Darius signed the writing and the decree. Now when Daniel knew that the writing was signed, he went into his house; and his windows being open in his chamber toward Jerusalem, he kneeled upon his knees three times a day, and prayed, and gave thanks before his God, as he did aforetime.... Then they came near, and spake before the king concerning the king's decree; Hast thou not signed a decree, that every man that shall ask a petition of any God or man within thirty days, save of thee, O king, shall be cast into the den of lions? The king answered and said, The thing is true, according to the law of the Medes and Persians, which altereth not."*

Scripture emphasizes how the decree could not be altered or reversed once the writing was signed. In Daniel 6:14-15, the text teaches how the king himself wanted to reverse the *dat* (decree), but it could not be changed. Daniel 6:14-15 tells us, *"Then the king, when he heard these words, was sore displeased with himself, and set his heart on Daniel to deliver him: and he laboured till the going down of the sun to deliver him. Then these men assembled unto the king, and said unto the king, Know, O king, that the law of the Medes and Persians is, That no decree nor statute which the king establisheth may be changed."*

The Blood Bought Blessing That Will Reverse The Adverse in Your Life

In Colossians 2, we see that the blood of Christ blotted out the handwriting of ordinances that was against us. Colossians 2:14 says, *"Blotting out the handwriting of ordinances that was against us, which was contrary to us, and took it out of the way, nailing it to his cross."*

This means that whatever has been used by the wicked one to stop, hinder, or destroy your destiny has been disannulled by the blood of Christ. In the book of Esther, the decree of wicked Haman had no power, because another decree was written that was higher than the one Haman had written. As we explore how the decree was disannulled, we will understand how through Christ we have been given Purim power to undo demonic decrees and assignments over our lives.

First, let us see God's promise about how He shall deliver us from the dat. In Isaiah 28:18a, the text teaches that *"your covenant with death shall be disannulled, and your agreement with hell shall not stand."*

In Esther 8, there is a supernatural similitude that prophetically prefigures how ungodly agreements and demonic decrees are broken. An ungodly agreement is a stronghold created by an evil conspiracy to destroy God's purpose in your life.

Psalm 83:5 says, *"For they have consulted together with one consent: they are confederate against thee."* This verse shows us how an ungodly agreement is like a confederacy against God's people.

Similarly, Psalm 62:4 says, *"They only consult to cast him down from his excellency: they delight in lies: they bless with their mouth, but they curse inwardly."* The psalmist in Psalm 62:4 teaches us that there is an ungodly agreement that is designated to cast us down from our place of excellence, which is our highest destiny.

The Anointing of Agreement in Heavenly Places in Christ

In the book of Esther, the text teaches us prophetic principles that help us understand how we disannul a strong demonic decree. I believe it is very important that we read how Esther carefully prepared her petition to the king when she asked him to reverse the curse of the ungodly death decree against the Jewish people.

Esther 8:3-5 says, *"And Esther spake yet again before the king, and fell down at his feet, and besought him with tears to put away the mischief of Haman the Agagite, and his device that he had devised against the Jews. Then the king held out the golden sceptre toward Esther. So Esther arose, and stood before the king, And said, If it please the king, and if I have favour in his sight, and the thing seem right before the king, and I be pleasing in his eyes, let it be written to reverse the letters devised by Haman the son of Hammedatha the Agagite, which he wrote to destroy the Jews which are in all the king's provinces."*

Surprisingly, although the golden scepter was extended to Esther, the king did not reverse the decree (although

Purim is a festival of divine reversal). Instead, the king reversed the power structure and took off the ring he had taken from Haman and gave it to Mordecai. We see in Esther 8:2 that *"the king took off his ring, which he had taken from Haman, and gave it unto Mordecai. And Esther set Mordecai over the house of Haman."*

Then the king gave both Mordecai and Esther the power to write their own decree, and the king sealed it. Esther 8:8 says, *"Write ye also for the Jews, as it liketh you, in the king's name, and seal it with the king's ring: for the writing which is written in the king's name, and sealed with the king's ring, may no man reverse."*

Both Mordecai and Esther writing their decree prophetically prefigures the agreement of two who have taken their position of authority and have been seated in heavenly places in Christ. Ephesians 2:6 tells us that God *"hath raised us up together, and made us sit together in heavenly places in Christ Jesus."*

Esther and Mordecai prophetically prefigure two united together in fasting and prayer, who have one heart and one mind, determined unto the death for the victory.

Esther 4:1-2 says, *"When Mordecai perceived all that was done, Mordecai rent his clothes, and put on sackcloth with ashes, and went out into the midst of the city, and cried with a loud and a bitter cry; And came even before the king's gate: for none might enter into the king's gate clothed with sackcloth."*

Esther 4:15-17 continues, *"Then Esther bade them return Mordecai this answer, Go, gather together all the Jews that are present in Shushan, and fast ye for me, and neither eat nor drink three days, night or day: I also and my maidens will fast likewise; and so will I go in unto the king, which is not according to the law: and if I perish, I perish. So Mordecai went his way, and did according to all that Esther had commanded him."*

The agreement of Mordecai and Esther is a prophetic parallel of how united prayer fortifies the strength of the Spirit in unbeatable victory against our common foe. Scripture shows us how united agreement can overcome the enemy. Joshua 23:10a says, *"One man of you shall chase a thousand,"* and Deuteronomy 32:30 says, *"How should one chase a thousand, and two put ten thousand to flight, except their Rock had sold them, and the Lord had shut them up?"*

Mordecai and Esther prophetically prefigure the anointing of agreement in the church that has the power to break demonic decrees and devices assigned against our destinies when we are of one heart and mind. Just as Mordecai and Esther were kin of the royal bloodline of King Saul, so we also share the same royal blood of

Christ who is our King; we are kin who have been redeemed by the blood and are of the same family. As Matthew 23:8b says, *"Ye all are brethren."*

Submissiveness to The Holy Spirit

In a supernatural sense of Scripture, Esther and Mordecai not only prophetically prefigure the unbreakable, undefeatable agreement of two sealed in heavenly places in Christ, but they also represent submissiveness to the Spirit. Esther and Mordecai demonstrated submissiveness to the Holy Spirit themselves, and they also represent those who submit to the role of the Spirit in His divine direction through prayer.

This prophetic picture is seen in the messenger Hatach and in Mordecai. Mordecai became a voice to Esther through the messenger Hatach. This is because the queen was in the palace and Mordecai was lying at the king's gate. Hatach is a prophetic prefiguring of the role of the Holy Spirit in our lives, who teaches us how to intercede according to the will of God. Both Mordecai and Hatach represent the role of the Holy Spirit in the life of an intercessor.

First, the name Hatach can be compared in concept to the Hebrew word *techinah* (Strong's Hebrew 8467). *Techinah* has within it the Hebrew word for favor (*chin*), which means to supplicate and receive favor. *Ha* is the Hebrew word for "the" and *tach* is an abbreviated form of *techinah*. Therefore, *ha tach* means "the request that incurs favor from God." Hatach, as a type of Holy Spirit, teaches us how to incur favor from God.

In Esther 4:9, the text goes out of its way to include the unusual information concerning the message and the messenger because Scripture is prophetically paralleling Hatach as a type of the Holy Spirit. Esther 4:9 says, *"Hatach came and told Esther the words of Mordecai."* Hatach prophetically prefigures how the Holy Spirit enables us to present our supplication to God and receive favor.

Second, Mordecai represents an additional work of the Spirit. If we venture out in prayer with our own thoughts or our own ways, we could miss the mark. Scripture teaches us clearly that we do not know how to pray as we ought, but the Spirit himself helps us in this area. Romans 8:26-27 says, *"Likewise the Spirit also helpeth our infirmities: for we know not what we should pray for as we ought: but the Spirit itself maketh intercession for us with groanings which cannot be uttered. And he that searcheth the hearts knoweth what is the mind of the Spirit, because he maketh intercession for the saints according to the will of God."*

In this case, Esther needed direction. She was not intending to go in unto the king on behalf of her people because, first of all, she did not know of their plight as of yet. Esther 4:7-8 says, *"And Mordecai told him [Hatach] of all that had happened unto him, and of the sum of the money that Haman had promised to pay to the king's treasuries for the Jews, to destroy them. Also he gave him the copy of the writing of the decree that was given at Shushan to destroy them, to shew it unto Esther, and to declare it unto her, and to charge her that she should go in unto the king, to make supplication unto him, and to make request before him for her people."*

Additionally, Esther was not even thinking of risking her life since a decree had been established that anyone who dared go before the king without being called after a 30-day period would be executed. Esther 4:11 says, *"All the king's servants, and the people of the king's provinces, do know, that whosoever, whether man or women, shall come unto the king into the inner court, who is not called, there is one law of his to put him to death, except such to whom the king shall hold out the golden sceptre, that he may live: but I have not been called to come in unto the king these thirty days."*

Mordecai is also an archetype of the role of the Holy Spirit in our lives as the one who strengthens and assists us with His heavenly help. The text teaches that Mordecai sent a message through Hatach (remember that both Mordecai and Hatach represent the role of the Spirit in prayer). The message sent by Mordecai to Esther included strong guidance on how to respond to what she knew by then to be true. His guidance was the most critical component of victory in the entire battle. Had Esther not responded to the correction and direction that Mordecai gave her, she surely would have failed and lost her destiny forever.

Beloved, this is why we need the Holy Spirit more than the breath we breathe. This shows how our victory depends completely on our yieldedness to the Holy Spirit. If we follow our own thoughts or our own ways, we are sunk. We must be totally dependent upon Him and yield ourselves to His promptings of power.

Let's take a look at the words Mordecai sent to Esther through Hatach. Esther 4:13-14 says, *"Then Mordecai commanded to answer Esther, Think not with thyself that thou shalt escape in the king's house, more than all the Jews. For if thou altogether holdest thy peace at this time, then shall there enlargement and deliverance arise to the Jews from another place; but thou and thy father's house shall be destroyed: and who knoweth whether thou art come to the kingdom for such a time as this?"*

Beloved, these words led Esther to respond with the type of attitude and intention that defeats demonic power. Her response was not one of double mindedness. She did not procrastinate. She immediately yielded her entire self. Through this, she became a weapon of war against Amalek.

Dedication Unto Death

Mordecai, a perfect type of the Holy Spirit, gave Esther instructions on how to step into God's divine design of destiny for her life. The words he spoke were prophetically paralleled to the way the Holy Spirit always leads His children. The path He offers to us is always a path of power. It is the path of total surrender of self and will to God. He will always offer us the cross. If we follow that path the way Esther surrendered herself to the words of Mordecai, so shall we step into the highest dimension of destiny for our lives.

Matthew 16:24-26 tells us, *"Then said Jesus unto his disciples, If any man will come after me, let him deny himself, and take up his cross, and follow me. For whosoever will save his life shall lose it: and whosoever will lose his life for my sake shall find it. For what is a man profited, if he shall gain the whole world, and lose his own soul? or what shall a man give in exchange for his soul?"*

Mordecai gave Esther the advice to lay her life down unto the death. He knew God was giving her the opportunity to be the vessel that God had chosen to deliver His people at that moment. He also told her that her willingness to be faithful unto death would result in a destiny. Esther 4:14b says, *"and who knoweth whether thou art come to the kingdom for such a time as this."* Refusal to heed this call, however, would mean that God would choose another way or another person to deliver the Jews. To Esther, the results of such a disastrous decision would mean a complete denial of destiny forever.

Esther 4:14a says, *"For if thou altogether holdest thy peace at this time, then shall there enlargement and deliverance arise to the Jews from another place; but thou and thy father's house shall be destroyed."*

Let us ask the Holy Spirit to speak to us as Mordecai spoke to Esther. Let us ask Him to reveal any areas of our lives that are not surrendered unto the death to do the will of God. In doing so, the diadem of destiny awaits us. When we say "Yes," we pay the price through complete surrender of self and find the treasure of the kingdom, as well our preordained place in the kingdom.

In her dedication unto death, Esther became the weapon of war that would disannul the decree. Revelation 12:11 says, *"And they overcame him by the blood of the Lamb, and by the word of their testimony; and they loved not their lives unto the death."*

Beloved, let us completely surrender ourselves to the will of God and become the weapons of war that He has called us to be!

Prayer

Dear Jesus,

I ask You to help me see the role of the Holy Spirit in my life. I know it is through Him that my supplication will find favor in heaven. I ask You for the grace to submit my entire self to Him the way Esther submitted herself in obedience to Mordecai. Give me grace through the provision of power that You have granted me through the Holy Spirit. I request that I be faithful and dedicated unto death. Amen!

Diary for Destiny

1. Are there areas of your life where you feel the Holy Spirit calling you to a greater surrender of self? Have you said "Yes" to the Lord in every area of your life?

2. Are there areas of your life that are difficult for you to surrender? If so, why? Are you afraid of God's will? Invite the Lord to increase your willingness to fully surrender these areas!

Chapter Five

The Anointing: Tranformation for Highest Manifestation of Destiny

An Experience In the Megillah Through the Eyes of Esther:

GO TO YOURSELF (Lech Lecha)

I will never forget the day when I was suddenly called out of the house of women. I had spent several months there learning about the protocol of the palace and of the royal court, while also being prepared with oils. The oils reminded me of the stories I had heard as a child, while sitting on the lap of my beloved cousin Mordecai. As Mordecai taught me Torah, he read to me from *Sefer Shmuel* (book of 1 Samuel) about our ancestor, Shaul, the first *melech* (king) of Israel. I remember distinctly when my cousin taught me about how Shaul was anointed. It seemed so real I could almost touch the oil. I became intrigued by seeing my cousin's eyes on fire as his beard rubbed against my face. He used a long instrument as he pointed to the holy words (*lashon hakodesh*) in the scroll of *Shmuel HaNavi* (the prophet Samuel).

As I went through the purification process with the other women, I felt my body was being permeated for something more than beauty alone. My *neshama* (soul) was being awakened and anointed with *malchut* (kingliness) for a destiny beyond my understanding. Every day when the oils dripped to my feet and were smeared across my face by the maidservants, I closed my eyes and lifted a *tefillah* (prayer) to Hashem. I remembered the *brachah* (blessing) my beloved cousin had pronounced over me before I was taken to this place. I knew these oils were transforming my soul and awakening within me the reality of my heritage as the great-great-grandaughter of King Shaul. Though separated from my people in the house of women, I felt as if I was being united to Rachel, Joseph, and Benjamin for some great purpose to glorify my God.

During those days, although I suffered excruciating loneliness, I felt the safe *chesed* (loving-kindness) of my God. It was there in those dark days that His love was stirred up within me and compelled me to give it to others. There were so many young women so lost, alone, and hurt. With joy my daily task became one of wiping their tears and holding them in my arms. I wanted to make them feel safe. While in the house of women, I also experienced days of isolation. I longed for my people but I could not even speak of them, for my beloved cousin had commanded me to not reveal my identity or my people. Something within me knew that my destiny and my purpose was connected to my willingness to obey the one Hashem had placed over my life.

As the days passed, I found that the times of *Pesach* (Passover), *Shavuot* (Pentecost), and our other holy days were extremely difficult, because I wanted to observe the feast days with my people. I recall one time during Passover that was especially difficult. I wanted to observe *Pesach* (Passover) with my people. I wanted to tell all of those who had never known the name of my God about the way He delivered our people from Mitzrayim. I had no *matzah* (unleavened bread) or *maror* (bitter herbs) for a Pesach meal, so I gave thanks to my God in the secret of my soul.

I prayed, "Oh Hashem, God of my fathers, feed me with the holy *matzah* of unleavened bread. Deliver our people from this *galut* (exile). Restore the ruins of Yerushalayim. Remember your promise to our *avot* (fathers), and bring us back to the holy *eretz* (land)."

The days of loneliness continued. Then suddenly one day, during the tenth month of Tevet, in the seventh year of the reign of the king, expecting the morning to be in the usual customary procedure of the day, I heard a train of footsteps quickly approaching in the corridor. There were menservants and maidservants, and also the seven chamberlains of the king along with other officials whom I could not identify, who came suddenly for me. It happened so quickly that I had no time to prepare. I felt like my ancestor Joseph, who was called out of the prison on the day that he appeared before Pharaoh. I remember my beloved cousin telling me that on the same day that our ancestor Joseph was called out of prison, the king put the ring upon his finger and made him ruler over Egypt.

As the multitude quickly approached my veiled chamber, Hege the chamberlain hastened to the forefront. He seemed frantic, which almost frightened me. Immediately I thought, "Is there a decree *(dat)*? Is it now going to affect my life? Why did they come for me?"

Hege said, "Esther, someone is watching over you. Come with me and get everything you have acquired in this place, for you will not be returning."

I had no time to say goodbye to my dear little sisters. As they saw me frantically gathering my garments and few possessions, especially the ones that Cousin Mordecai had given me that were so dear to my heart, some ran up and embraced me, while others said, "Remember us, O Esther!" We hurried across the palace gardens, and I realized that we were out of the court of women. To my utter amazement stood four men clad in royal apparel. They were standing at attention under a canopy laden with jewels and the finest Persian tapestry. There was also a bed laden with peacock feathers waiting for the one destined to be escorted to the palace.

My dear Hege instructed me, "Esther, when you arrive at the palace, your maidservant will dress you quickly, for all the kings' servants and royal attendants and all of the governors from all the provinces have been summoned to the banquet this night."

After we entered the palace, I was taken to an area where I could be readied for the banquet. I could smell the sweet spices and feel the change of temperature as I approached the steaming baths. Immediately I was covered in oils and sweet spices. I whispered a prayer to my God, "Oh Hashem, I believe I know what is happening. I did not choose this, but You chose it for me. I ask, my God, that You keep me as the apple of Your eye. As this oil is poured on my head, let it be an anointing. Let Your *chesed* be extended to the house of my father King Shaul, whose descendant I am. Let my life be given as a *korban* (sacrifice) for *Beit ha Israel* (the house of Israel). Let these be as the very oils and spices You commanded for the *shemen* (oil) upon our kings. Let me bring a restoration to the house of my fathers." I was then quickly girded with queenly attire including a heavy jeweled robe. Immediately I was whisked into the banquet hall of the palace, where the sounds of trumpets and timbrels and shouts could be heard. There were numerous persons of every province decked in attire for the royal banquet. The outer courts were decorated with tapestries of every color, and the smells of delicacies filled the air.

Then, as the trumpets sounded, came a servant holding a crown on a decorated case. He bowed before me and shouted, "Give honor to the queen of Persia, Queen Esther of the Achaemenid Empire!"

Stepping Stones Into Greatness:

How God Uses Pain to Train for Greatness

Once I heard Kathryn Kuhlman say that God uses the most unlikely people, those who are most unqualified in the natural. Who would ever imagine that a girl who was an orphan would be called to destroy Amalek, the archenemy of Israel? Is there a difference between Hadassah and Esther? In a personal prophetic sense of Scripture, the name Hadassah prophetically parallels how God will bring transformation to our human limitation. 1 Corinthians 2:16 says, *"For who hath known the mind of the Lord, that he may instruct him? But we have the mind of Christ."*

One of the supernatural secrets to understanding the book of Esther is understanding the command regarding the destruction of Amalek. The command to annihilate Amalek was previously given to King Saul, Esther's ancestor. The Bible introduces us to King Saul by telling us about his exceptional extraordinary qualities. Scripture goes out of its way to inform us that he is more than qualified to fulfill the commandment to blot out the remembrance of Amalek from under heaven. If we were to assess the assets of any individual in the Bible to see who would be the most preferred individual to annihilate Amalek, the choice would be Saul.

Let's take a look at what God's Word teaches us about Saul's external qualifications. 1 Samuel 10:23-24 says, *"And they ran and fetched him thence: and when he stood among the people, he was higher than any of the people from his shoulders and upward. And Samuel said to all the people, See ye him whom the Lord hath chosen, that there is none like him among all the people? And all the people shouted, and said, God save the king."*

Scripture is letting us know that Saul had everything necessary to ensure he would not fail in his assignment. First, he had reputation. 1 Samuel 9:1-2 says, *"Now there was a man of Benjamin, whose name was Kish, the son of Abiel, the son of Zeror, the son of Bechorath, the son of Aphiah, a Benjamite, a mighty man of power. And he had a son, whose name was Saul, a choice young man, and a goodly: and there was not among the children of Israel a goodlier person than he: from his shoulders and upward he was higher than any of the people."*

Second, he had impartation. 1 Samuel 10:1, 6 tells us, *"Then Samuel took a vial of oil, and poured it upon his*

[Saul's] head, and kissed him, and said, Is it not because the Lord hath anointed thee to be captain over his inheritance? ... And the Spirit of the Lord will come upon thee, and thou shalt prophesy with them, and shalt be turned into another man." 1 Samuel 10:10 continues, *"And when they came thither to the hill, behold, a company of prophets met him [Saul]; and the Spirit of God came upon him, and he prophesied among them."*

Third, he had physical qualification. 1 Samuel 10:23 says, *"And they ran and fetched him thence: and when he stood among the people, he was higher than any of the people from his shoulders and upward."* Saul was recognized as a "giant" among the people.

Scripture documents these details so we would know there is no justifiable reason why he could not perform the commandment of the Lord. Saul was equipped to carry out his calling, but he did not complete the assignment. So his descendant Esther, even though she was a woman and an orphan, had to fulfill what Saul forfeited.

The question is, how did this little girl named Hadassah become Esther anyway? Is Esther just an alias or an alternate name for Hadassah?

In Esther, Chapters 2 through 4, Scripture shows us the secret of destiny that lies within the two names. The name Esther indicates a transformation from limitation, while the name Hadassah represents the pain of the past that keeps us stuck in strongholds.

In a theological sense of Scripture, this concept is conveyed in the use of the terms "Esther" and "Esther the queen." The phrase "Esther the queen" is not used in the text until after she is willing to lay her life down unto the death for her people.

If we make an analysis of the *megillah* (scroll or book) of Esther, we see that Mordecai, the author of the book of Esther, deliberately never uses the royal title "Esther the queen" until Esther 5:2. Let us take a look at this unique transitional text. It becomes very apparent that he uses the name Esther but does not reveal to us that she is Esther the queen until she has made the decision that could cost her life.

Esther 5:2 says, *"And it was so, when the king saw Esther the queen standing in the court, that she obtained favor in his sight: and the king held out to Esther the golden scepter that was in his hand. So Esther drew near, and touched the top of the scepter."*

We see in Esther 4, especially verses 9 through 11, that Esther still thinks like Hadassah in many ways and has not yet fully stepped into the experience of transformation for the highest manifestation of predestined purpose. Hadassah is passive and understands that even though she is the queen, it is against culture and law for a woman in the Persian Empire to make any decisions or voice any opinions that would be interpreted as brash. Acting like the brazen, bold Vashti, who refused to come at the king's command, could lead to dire consequences.

Not only is Hadassah in nature very careful to always comply, but she also had strong anxieties and fears, because for 30 days she had not been called into the king's presence. For the Medes and the Persians, 30 days was not just a length of time that seems to indicate an absence of affection. A period of 30 days seems to be connected with strong political and social implications for those in close contact with the affairs of the king.

As in all books of the Bible, particular junctures and compositional structures must be interpreted through intertextuality. This means that when we come to an unusual place within the text or critical questions arise regarding the action of a certain individual, we search for words or phrases found in other *seforim* (books) of the *Tanakh* (Bible) that will help us to understand the author's intent.

In Esther 4:9-11, we encounter such a juncture. The question is, why does Hadassah respond to Mordecai's request, given to her through Hatach, with an excuse of why she cannot go before the king and make supplication for her people?

For context, let's look at Esther 4:8-11 as Mordecai commands Hatach to give Esther this order. Esther 4:8-11 says, *"Also he [Mordecai] gave him [Hatach] the copy of the writing of the decree that was given at Shushan to destroy them, to shew it unto Esther, and to declare it unto her, and to charge her that she should go in unto the king, to make supplication unto him, and to make request before him for her people. And Hatach came and told Esther the words of Mordecai. Again Esther spake unto Hatach, and gave him commandment unto Mordecai; All the king's servants, and the people of the king's provinces, do know, that whosoever, whether man or women, shall come unto the king into the inner court, who is not called, there is one law of his to put him to death, except such to whom the king shall hold out the golden scepter, that he may live: but I have not been called to come in unto the king these thirty days."*

Esther's response in Esther 4:11 is completely unlike her obedient, unselfish personality. In Esther 2:10 and Esther 2:20, the text teaches us about her most valuable character trait: obedience. It is the character trait that God so honored that He promoted her to the position of queen. This particular character trait is a contingency for her destiny.

Everything in Esther's life synthesized together by the power of divine providence to formulate this outstanding character trait within her. Every aspect of her childhood suffering and the tender loving fatherly care given to her by Mordecai molded within her this *middah* (character trait). This character trait of obedience is the jewel in the diadem of her destiny.

Esther 2:10 says, *"Esther had not shewed her people nor her kindred: for Mordecai had charged her that she should not shew it."* Even after she became queen, Esther remained faithful, humble, submissive, and obedient to Mordecai. She carefully followed all of his instructions with complete equanimity, not being swayed by position or power. Scripture shows that Esther is established in obedience and that this character trait gives definition to her destiny.

So why has Esther responded so out of her heroic character by very politely using protocol as the excuse for not going before the king?

When we come to this critical place, the 30-day period seems to be the key. Using intertextuality will give us a more complete composite of why there is an apparent crisis in the consistency of her character. This is written not to show us any character flaw in our heroic queen, but to teach us the degree of dedication that is going to be required of her.

The situation is compared in context to Daniel 6. Like Esther and Mordecai, Daniel lived in exile under the rule of the Medes and Persians. In Daniel 6, Daniel was confronted with a law that would be enforced for 30 days.

Daniel 6:7 says, *"All the presidents of the kingdom, the governors, and the princes, the counsellors, and the captains, have consulted together to establish a royal statute, and to make a firm decree, that whosoever shall ask a petition of any God or man for thirty days, save of thee, O king, he shall be cast into the den of lions."* It appears that when a law was enforced for 30 days, it became a decree. In the land of the Medes and the Persians, not all commands of the king were considered to be decrees. A decree was a law that could never be reversed, altered, or changed.

Esther's response to Mordecai reveals her anxiety and fear of the *dat* (decree), because she remembered the dat that had been written against Vashti. Once again, Esther 4:11 tells us, *"All the king's servants, and the people of the king's provinces, do know, that whosoever, whether man or women, shall come unto the king into the inner court, who is not called, there is one law of his to put him to death, except such to whom the king shall hold out the golden scepter, that he may live: but I have not been called to come in unto the king these thirty days."*

Beloved, we must understand that 30 days does not indicate a lonely queen who feels rejected from her king. It is much more than that. A 30-day represents the possibility of a death decree.

Scripture wants us to understand that Hadassah does not become Esther the queen until she is willing to make a definite decision unto death.

John 12:24-25 says, *"Verily, verily, I say unto you, Except a corn of wheat fall into the ground and die, it abideth alone: but if it die, it bringeth forth much fruit. He that loveth his life shall lose it; and he that hateth his life in this world shall keep it unto life eternal."*

After Esther tries to explain why she cannot go before the king, Mordecai rebukes her. Esther 4:13-14 tells us, *"Then Mordecai commanded to answer Esther, Think not with thyself that thou shalt escape in the king's house, more than all the Jews. For if thou altogether holdest thy peace at this time, then shall there enlargement and deliverance arise to the Jews from another place; but thou and thy father's house shall be destroyed: and who knoweth whether thou art come to the kingdom for such a time as this."*

Esther humbly recognized the *tochachah* (correction) of Mordecai concerning taking the responsibility of her God-given position. Esther quickly responded, knowing that God had given her such a high place and position not for her own benefit, but for the benefit of her people. Esther was also well aware that her great ancestor King Saul did not fulfill what he had been called to do, and she was sensitive to overcoming her own internal issues and the family tendency toward disobedience.

Mordecai's correction compelled Esther into purpose. A true champion is known by facing great opposition that God uses to position for greatness. With her heart racing and fears pressing, Esther knew there was no other way to save her people. The clock was ticking with only days to resolve a catastrophe that was imminent. Moments would make the difference between a people whose greatness would continue to the end of time, or who would become a breath that faded in the wind.

But how could Esther break the bond between that wicked Haman and the king? Haman had manipulated and dominated the king by a bribe. The king was intoxicated but not with wine. The king had become bewitched by a bribe of 10,000 talents of silver for the sale of the Jewish people.

Esther fasted and sought the Lord for three days, inquiring of the Lord about how to overthrow Haman's plot. Not eating, not drinking, barely sleeping, and constantly praying, Hadassah (that is, Esther) arose from the dust and donned her royal robes as Esther the queen. She was determined to approach the king and intercede for the lives of her people, no matter the cost. It was this decision unto death that opened the door to her destiny.

As Esther made her approach to the inner court where the king sat on his throne, she could not allow her thoughts to be filled with fear about the *dat* (decree). Though strikingly stunning, Esther knew her beauty could not calm the beast. For who had been more alluring and fair to behold than Vashti?

Instead, Esther called to mind the heroism of her ancestors Yochabed and Miriam (also known as Puah and Shifra) who dared defy the law of Pharaoh to save the Hebrew children. Esther was convinced that with the help of the Almighty, her willingness unto death would overturn the decree. If God did it then, He would surely do it again. Esther's love for God gave her power over passivity. Hadassah – that is, Esther – had transitioned and become fully positioned as Esther the queen. Her life teaches us that the only way of going to our true self is by losing ourselves for others and the sake of heaven.

Esther 5:2 says, *"And it was so, when the king saw Esther the queen standing in the court, that she obtained favor in his sight: and the king held out to Esther the golden scepter that was in his hand. So Esther drew near, and touched the top of the scepter."*

Beloved, let us allow the Lord to transform us into greatness so that we can fulfill our destinies!

Prayer

Lord, You have blessed me to be a blessing to others, and have uniquely placed me "for such a time as this." Show me how to use the position and gifts that You have given me for Your glory. Transform me into a person of greatness, and let me not be afraid of losing my life. Help me to always be obedient to You, no matter the cost. In the name of Jesus, amen!

Diary for Destiny

1. Hadassah had great obedience and compassion, but needed to overcome fear and passivity in order to transform into Esther the queen. What are the strengths of your personality? And what are some of the personality challenges that you need to overcome in order to transform into greatness? Invite the Lord to transform you into the fullness of who He has called you to be!

2. We may be called to make the ultimate sacrifice and lay down our lives in order to do what God is calling us to do. But many times we have to "die to self" and sacrifice something else such as our pride or position when we follow the Lord. Is God calling you to do something that might lead to actual death or "dying to

self"? Describe the situation, and ask the Lord to help you follow His perfect will for your life!

Chapter Six

The Supernatural Secret of Malchut

An Experience In the Megillah Through the Eyes of Esther:

THE ANOINTING AND APPOINTING FOR DESTINY

It was five years after my coronation as the queen of the empire, in the twelfth year of King Ahasuerus' reign, that I understood the infernal wickedness of Haman, one of the king's highest-ranking officials. Haman, the embodiment of evil, cast *pur* against *Am Israel* (the people of Israel) to determine a date for our destruction. Who would dare be so brazen as to not fear the mighty God of Israel who had split the Red Sea and brought down the empire of Egypt? But as a true Amalekite descendant of the royal seed of King Agag, Haman cast *pur* against Am Israel, trusting only in chance, coincidence, sorcery, and other means that are an abomination to our God and to our people.

As I was shut away in my royal quarters, I had no idea of the sorrow, suffering, wailing, and crying that was going on outside the walls of Shushan the palace. Hatach my servant brought me word of my cousin Mordecai's unusual cries at the king's gate. He said that Mordecai had been covered with dust and was crying out prayers in Hebrew night and day, wailing without end. I could not imagine why my beloved cousin, a dignified servant of the king, would behave in such a manner. I hurriedly sent Hatach to inquire *Lama* (Why?) my dear cousin was acting this way.

Immediately Cousin Mordecai sent me back an urgent order demanding that I act at once, that I go before the king and plead for the lives of my people. Mordecai had also sent me a copy of the dat that had been written and posted throughout the empire. This dat was a royal decree that could not be reversed. On the thirteenth day of the Biblical month of Adar, every Jew in the kingdom of King Ahasuerus would be killed, annihilated, and destroyed. Even women and small children, all Jews no matter who they were, great or small, were subject to this decree of death.

I immediately returned a message to Mordecai through my servant Hatach, saying that everyone among the king's servants knew that anyone who appeared before the king after 30 days of not being called was subject to death. I informed Mordecai that I had not been called before the king for 30 days, and reminded him that the only one who would escape death was the one to whom the king would stretch out his royal scepter.

My beloved cousin, whom I had been taught to obey since the time that I was a child, whom I had never disobeyed under any conditions, then gave me the most difficult order of my life. The words of my cousin came back to me with severe warning, telling me that if I didn't speak up at this time, then God would deliver the people of Israel in another way, but that I and my father's house would perish.

I had always obeyed my cousin Mordecai. I truly believe that my testing ground was when he had commanded me to never say that I was a Jew during the entire time that I was being trained in Shushan the palace with Hege. If I had kept silent under such difficult circumstances and obeyed the word that my beloved cousin, my teacher of Torah, had given me back then, should I not obey now? Didn't Hashem protect me back then when I could have lost my life for not revealing my identity?

But this test seemed more severe than that previous test. The words of my beloved cousin came back to me with severe warning, almost like the way that the prophet Samuel had spoken to Shaul. Would I respond as my ancestor Shaul? Would I disobey the command of the one that God had put over me? Would I fall into the same deplorable sin that my ancestor had fallen into when he became so prideful that he no longer obeyed the one that God had placed over his life? I recalled the words of the prophet Samuel when he spoke to my ancestor, *Shaul HaMelech* (King Saul): "When you were little in your own sight, were you not made captain over all the tribes of Israel?" But over time Shaul had fallen from that posture of humility to one of disobedience and pride.

"Oh, Hashem," I wondered, "have I fallen into the same sin?" At that moment, I resolved within my heart that I would not do what Shaul had done. I would follow through and obey my God. I knew that I had not become queen for my own benefit. I was placed here by the power of divine providence. This was my opportunity to stand up against the Amalekites, to go and to plead for the lives of my people. It was also a diadem that heaven was offering me to restore *malchut* (kingship) to the house of my fathers.

Stepping Stones Into Greatness:

From Self-Negation into Highest Exaltation

Have you ever wondered how Esther achieved such an exalted state of position and power? We must note that throughout the Bible the text teaches there is no such thing as a "free pass" to greatness.

Is it a proper assessment to think that Esther became queen because of her beauty alone? Certainly we know that she was beautiful, but God and not man made the decision for Esther to become queen. So what is the "success secret" that qualified Esther in God's eyes to become queen? Similarly, when we behold the exaltedness of David, Joseph, Ruth, and Esther, we may ask the question, "How did that happen?" You may even wonder, "Could that level of promotion ever occur in my own life?"

The Bible documents the details of these individuals' rise to greatness in a narrative form, not as a history lesson, but in order to instruct us. Every narrative contains life lessons that will shift us into our highest purpose and promise. Everyone in the Bible that has reached the pinnacle of their highest destiny has possessed the character trait of *malchut*. Malchut is kingliness, kingship, or kingdom.

Dear beloved friend, the path to greatness includes having heroic, virtuous character traits like *chesed* (loving-kindness) and the quality of *tamimus* (blamelessness), which is the contingency for covenant. Blamelessness in a nutshell is purity of heart and integrity or uprightness. God told Abraham before he experienced the exaltedness of the fullness of destiny and promise in his life that blamelessness or the character trait of *tamimus* would be the prerequisite for possessing the promises of his highest potential and purpose. This is illustrated in Genesis 17:1, when God said to Abraham, *"I am the Almighty God [El Shaddai]. Walk before Me, and be thou perfect."*

The word "perfect" in English translates in Hebrew to the word *tam* (denoting *tamimus*). It was after Abram was fully tested in every area of his character that he arrived at the place of his spiritual destination, which was to be the father of many nations. Genesis 12:1-3 shows us the promise and destiny that God had for Abram: "*Now the Lord had said unto Abram, Get thee out of thy country, and from thy kindred, and from thy father's house, unto a land that I will shew thee: And I will make of thee a great nation, and I will bless thee, and make thy name great; and thou shalt be a blessing: And I will bless them that bless thee, and curse him that curseth thee: and in thee shall all families of the earth be blessed.*" This promise was obtained through the process of developing character to its highest potential, which is *malchut*. It was only after this series of testings when the quality of Abram's character had been proven that God changed his name from Abram to Abraham.

The text teaches us in Genesis 12:1 to Genesis 17:5 (five chapters) that Abram experienced specific tests and training to lift his all of his *middot* (character traits) to the level where he could achieve malchut. We also see that the great mission of the *avot* (the fathers) was to set forth the destiny of all their descendants toward the same calling of greatness. God told Jacob in Genesis 46:3b to *"fear not to go down to Mitzrayim (Egypt), for there I will make of thee a great nation [or people]."*

We see in Genesis 12 that Abraham endured the very essential test of going down into *Mitzrayim* (Egypt), and came out with exceedingly great substance and riches (Genesis 13:1-2). This test was essential because it would stand as a promise to his future descendants that they would also go down into *Mitzrayim* (Egypt) because of a famine, and just like Abraham come out with great substance (Genesis 15:13-14). In Genesis 13, we see one of Abraham's greatest tests in the pathway of obtaining *malchut* (greatness). Abraham experienced a difficult dilemma to prove that his character was absolutely blameless before God. It was a very difficult test with his beloved nephew Lot, who was like a son to Abraham. Lot was the son of Abraham's brother Haran who had died (Genesis 11:28). Because of *chesed* (loving-kindness), the overall greatest character trait that Abraham possessed, Abraham took Lot his nephew and raised him as his own.

The text teaches us in Genesis 13:3 that Abraham went up into the land of Canaan after he had left Egypt (moving to the land of Israel is known as making an *aliyah*). During this time there was strife between the herdsmen of Abram's cattle and the herdsmen of Lot's cattle (Genesis 13:7). To Abraham, this was not a light thing. Strife was a wicked character trait that was not acceptable in the household of Abraham. It interfered with the entire mission to spread *chesed* or loving-kindness throughout the land of Canaan. This strife also occurred because the herdsmen of Lot were not integrous. The herdsmen of Lot did not have a problem at all with their cattle grazing on the property of poor men, who are mentioned in Scripture as "the Canaanite and the Perizzite [who] dwelled in the land" (Genesis 13:7). The herdsmen of Abraham knew that their master would never allow even so much as a morsel that he did not pay for to be taken from another. His integrity or *tamimus* was of the highest level in all the land.

It was an essential part of Abraham's mission to be able to proclaim his God as the God of Abraham. In order to protect the name of God, Abraham had to make the very difficult decision to immediately part ways with his nephew who did not fully walk in the integrity that had been the hallmark of Abraham's household.

Abraham perceived that his mission to raise up the holiness of God, which in Hebrew is called raising the *kedushah*, could not be accomplished as long as Lot was part of his household. Notice how Scripture is teaching that this form of character development was an essential element in Abraham's highest dimension of destiny. Genesis 13:14-17 says, *"And the Lord said unto Abram, after that Lot was separated from him, Lift up now thine eyes, and look from the place where thou art northward, and southward, and eastward, and westward: For all the land which thou seest, to thee will I give it, and to thy seed for ever. And I will make thy seed as the dust of the earth: so that if a man can number the dust of the earth, then shall thy seed also be numbered. Arise, walk through the land in the length of it and in the breadth of it; for I will give it unto thee."* It was after Abraham had separated from Lot that God revealed His promises to Abraham.

Just as Abraham demonstrated the character trait of malchut, so also did David, Ruth, Joseph, Moses, Mordecai, Esther, and many others. In concept, malchut is a composite comprised of two distinct qualities. True malchut must have both of these qualities: *hitnasut* (exaltedness) and *shiflut* (humility).

Hitnasut means exaltedness. Sometimes this exaltedness (*hitnasut*) comes after great trials and tribulations. David depended on hitnasut as part of God's plan over his enemies. Psalm 25:2 says, *"Oh my God, I trust in thee, let not mine enemies triumph over me."* Psalm 41:11 states, *"By this I know that thou favorest me because mine enemy doth not triumph over me."* Throughout the psalms, David perceived the victories over his enemies as a reward for winning the inward battles of maintaining a pure heart and pure intentions (*kavanot*) and obtaining malchut.

The second quality necessary for malchut is *shiflut.* Shiflut is the quality of lowliness that esteems others better than one's self. Shiflut is humility that allows one to stay in an exalted position without arrogance, self-centeredness, and pride.

Malchut must be a combination of hitnasut and shiflut. The perfect example of true malchut tempered with the qualities of hitnasut and shiflut is found in 2 Samuel 5:12. The text teaches, *"And David knew that the Lord had established him as king over Israel and that He exalted his kingdom for His people Israel's sake."* David understood that he had been exalted to the position of king in order to bless, protect, and serve the people of Israel.

Similarly, the Bible shows us in Esther 2:20 that Esther maintained her exalted position as queen by keeping her heart in a place of *shiflut* (lowliness and humility). Esther 2:20 says, *"Esther had not yet shewed her kindred nor her people as Mordecai had charged her. For Esther kept the commandment of Mordecai like as when she was brought up by him."* Even after she became queen, Esther demonstrated the quality of shiflut by continuing to be obedient to her cousin Mordecai, who had raised her from her youth.

Beloved, let us aim to develop our character traits to the highest level and demonstrate the quality of malchut in our lives!

Prayer

Lord, thank you for helping us to develop the quality of malchut (kingliness) in our lives! Grant us hitnasut (exaltedness) and shiflut (humility) just like You did for Esther and David, so that we can sustain the highest calling on our lives and reach our destinies! In the name of Jesus, amen!

Diary for Destiny

1. In what ways have you demonstrated the quality of *malchut* (kingliness) in your life? Which areas of your character still need to improve in order for you to achieve malchut?

2. What are some practical steps that you can take to improve your character? Ask the Lord right now to give you grace and strength to keep improving your *middot* (character traits)!

Chapter Seven

Esther's Dream

An Experience In the Megillah Through the Eyes of Esther:

THE NEVUA OF ESTHER

(The Prophecy of Esther)

Immediately after I accepted full responsibility to defy the *dat* (decree) under penalty of execution in order to plead for the lives of my people, an overwhelming boldness arose over my soul. I felt a heavenly fire come down from *shamayim* (heaven). The flames were like liquid that did not consume me. As this fire fell upon me from *shamayim* (heaven), I became valiant and no longer afraid. Assistance came from heaven immediately upon my decision. The moment I resolved within my heart and became determined unto death, the fire fell upon me and enkindled my entire *neshama* (soul).

For a moment I had wrestled in my heart, recalling to mind Vashti's end and the *dat* (decree) that had been written against women as a result of her brazen resistance. Besides the *dat (*decree*)* that Memuchan (Haman) had devised against the women in order to suppress and repress the voice of women, there was also another decree. It was a decree that would result in the immediate death of any persons who would dare to go before the king with any petition or request if they had not been called by the king for 30 days.

The fierce and brutal giants of both decrees were a source of tyranny, coercing me to yield. I knew very well that my decision could cost me my life, should I dare present such a bold request that would appear to challenge the power of Haman and the decree he had devised against the Jews. Yet now I fully understood that I had arrived at this *malchut* (kingdom) for such a time as this. So much was at stake. Time was so short. Immediate and wise plans needed to be revealed from my God.

Though I defied the decree with every fiber of my being, I could not appear as if I found any fault in it. Doing that could backfire and the mission that I embarked upon could fail. The lives of our people, every Jew, depended upon how this was handled before our God. There indeed was a dilemma. It was not just boldness and willingness that was required – it was a plan. There had to be *machshava* (thought to devise). It had to be

Hashem's plan in the form of a disguise. It had to be something that Haman would never suspect. It had to appear passive and non-threatening. The plan required that I appear as if I were completely compliant to all of the orders of every *dat* (decree). I had such an overwhelming burden to save the lives of my people. But how could this plan possibly be accomplished with such short notice? The only way this could be discharged would be through supplicating to my God with a *nezer* (consecration).

The days of my *nezer* (consecration) began with three days of prayer and fasting. On the very first night, I did not want to even rest my head on a pillow. All I desired more than food and more than sleep was that my prayer would be a favorable supplication (*tekinah*) to my God. I pleaded with the One who hears the cry of the orphan (*yatom*).

On the second day, as I was beseeching my God for the plan to destroy Haman the Agagite of the seed of Amalek, I began to feel an unusual sleepiness that I could not fight. I felt like a whimpering child that finally shed its last tear before falling asleep. I drifted off into a deep sleep as I rested in the arms of my God.

While I was sleeping, I felt as if I was being taken to *shamayim* (heaven). Suddenly in my dream I began to hear strange sounds that I could not make out. They sounded like the trumpets sometimes heard in the Persian feasts. These sounds were not like our shofars. The sounds started very low and then went very high to a screeching pitch. I had never heard anything like these unusual sounds before, which seemed to be alarming sirens. These sirens seemed to put a sense of terror in the atmosphere. Then I beheld masses of people. There were women, and children being held by the hands of their mothers. I did not know these people. They were dressed very strangely, not like the people of Persia. I could see men clad in black coats which came to their knees. I could also see black hats on the men, which did not look like turbans. Then I saw women carrying their little ones, and wearing a small tapestry-type material over their heads. All of these people were going on a journey, being taken in a long caravan that looked like a box. There were so many people that I could not count them all, and there was no room for them in the place where they were being pushed and trampled, one upon another.

Then I saw other men with fierce faces. They had an unusual symbol upon their arms over their clothing. The symbol was just like the symbol of Amalek, clad on the garment of Haman. I felt a sense of deportation, just like I felt when I was brought on that dreadful day to Shushan the palace. But this seemed to be much more grievous, with cries, weeping, and wailing that could be heard in *shamayim* (heaven). It was the voice of Rachel crying for her children because they were no more. I knew these people were *Yehudim* (Jews). I could tell this because they all wore the same symbol on their clothing. It was the symbol of our national identity. All of *Yehudim* (Jews) since the time of *David HaMelech* (David the king) have worn this star. Where were they taking these people? Why was *Ima* (Mother) Rachel weeping with tears, refusing to be comforted?

Suddenly in my dream, there appeared the 10 sons of Haman. Near each one of the sons, there appeared an *eitz* (gallows). Hanging from the *eitz* (gallows) was an unusual symbol that was crooked in shape. Was it not the symbol of Amalek? This symbol was characterized by a crooked letter which was formed by two pieces that I had seen hanging from the gallows. It was the same symbol I had seen on the clothing of the cruel and vicious men who had forced the multitudes into the deportation.

The sense of alarm was everywhere. And much to my surprise, I could smell the smoke of a furnace. The smoke became stronger and stronger as it began to rise. I felt as if the furnace was prepared for the innocent. Was not this furnace the same fiery furnace that our father Abraham had seen in his dream when the Lord made a covenant with him and passed between the parts of Abraham's sacrifice? Our teacher *Moshe* (Moses) had written in *Bereshit* (Genesis) that Abraham, upon looking at the smoke coming up from the sacrifice, had fallen into a deep sleep, and a great horror of darkness had overwhelmed him. It was there that Hashem had given Abraham the promise that his seed would go down to *Mitzrayim* (Egypt) and come forth with great substance. But was this dream also speaking of something else? Where were our people going, and why did these vicious men wear on their clothing the symbol of Amalek?

To Be Continued....

~End of Book One~

Chesed Publications

What is Chesed?

Chesed means "loving kindness" in Hebrew. Our publication house is called Chesed Publishing because when you purchase a book, you are helping us to do the impossible for people that could never help themselves.

We provide daily feeding programs to orphans and grandmothers, pay for educational fees for children in our orphan homes, conduct medical missions throughout the world, purchase clean water wells, and so much more.

In April 2016, Chesed Publishing was founded to financially support Dr. Michelle Corral's vision of acts of chesed to the poor, along with the mission to pass on the wealth of teaching that God entrusted to her to the next generation.

Books Authored by Dr. Michelle Corral

Judgment
For
Jezebel

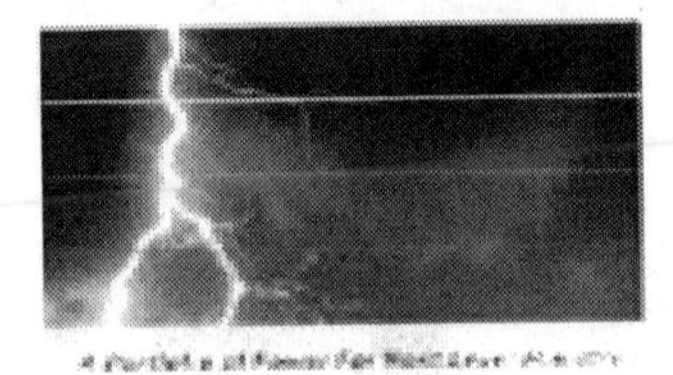

Coming Into Alignment Through

Character Refinement

Pathways Into Your Prophetic Purpose

Dr. Michelle Corral

For a Complete List of
CDs and Ministry Resources

Contact:
Breath of the Spirit Prophetic Word Center
P.O. BOX 2676
Orange, CA 92859
Phone # (714) 694-1100

Youtube.com/DrMichelleCorral
Word Network on Mondays
@ 10:30 pm PST

www.breathofthespirit.org
www.drmichellecorral.com
facebook.com/Dr.Corral

Made in the USA
San Bernardino, CA
21 June 2017